I Am Eternal; You Are Eternal

P Diane Chambers

"Our spirit knows we don't die nor are we born.
If our ego knew what our greater self knows,
it would not fear disaster...
Caught up in a new incarnation,
one may forget their Always State, Form;
perhaps forgetting everything from before.
However, one is already always that !
There is only eternity, knowledge and bliss !"

Kuan Yin

Rick —

Many

blessings and

great wellness to you ♡

P. Duane

Chamber

"Immortal is for the eternal soul and reality is for the
living body."

J. Nedumaan

Dedication

This book is dedicated to all the wonderful **healthcare folks** who have saved my sight and who have kept me alive. This book is dedicated to all of the **people** and **children I have loved**.

Jonathan L. Chambers, my son.

John (Johnny) D. Hess, my brother.

Dr. Julia A. Rosdahl - Duke Glaucoma Eye Surgeon.

Luke.

And to the wise old soul, **Mahatma Gandhi**.

Everyone wants to be heard and to be appreciated.
The cover of my book is a photo I took in my own yard.

Edited by **Jody Marmel** and **Dottie Davis**

You will notice that my book has double spacing between words also known as white spaces. I do this so that with my rare eye condition, I can read more easily. I have also left the white spaces to make others aware of folks, like me, with vision issues and folks with aging eyes. The double spacing is less tiresome to read.

Proceeds from this book will go to Digdeep.org -- *WATER IS LIFE* !!! There are 2.2 million Americans who still do not have running water in their homes. Much of the work of Dig Deep is in the Navajo and Appalachian areas of America. **Running water changes lives forever.**

I AM ETERNAL; YOU ARE ETERNAL

This is my true story. My life has been filled with great worrisome tribulations, countless frightening traumas, many medical dramas, and constant scary uncertainties. If you follow my journey, you will see how **gratitude conquers** and **inspires**. And if it changes your life while inspiring change in other people's lives at the same time, it truly is a rewarding journey for all of us. This is my story told from my heart.

I AM ETERNAL; YOU ARE ETERNAL

P Diane Chambers

Have you been to Heaven ?

I was there **six times** Valentine's Weekend 1998.

My **NEAR-DEATH EXPERIENCE** happened in 1998. In spite of my reluctance, I have decided to write about it now, at age 75 in 2022. I know so many who are grieving. This comes often with the losses of aging. I hope that my story will allow folks to find joy and comfort from their grief; and, will serve as a warning to some about reconsidering their choices. **We are all Eternal.** If you don't like what you read, perhaps it is time you take stock of your real values and align your standards.

Additionally, I have the rare condition of Autonomic Neuropathy - my nerves are destroying themselves. Mayo Clinic gives me about two to three more years. So, if I am going to share my story with others, I need to share it now. I have written about my experiences many times before, but only to myself.

"People are like books - some deceive you by their glossy cover and others surprise you by their deep content."
Harsh Goenka

Every time I see the title of my beloved Bernie Sanders' book THE FIGHTING SOUL - I think …. this is the story of my life also. As a man when you have a fighting spirit you are respected; as a woman you are avoided and ignored. Like Bernie Sanders, I **"ASPIRE to INSPIRE before I EXPIRE"**. Eugene Bell Jr. **JESUS WAS A FIGHTING SOUL** - trying to right the wrongs. Other older, wise souls have also tried to improve the world. I have always asked myself, *what would Jesus do.* As Gandhi said, "**Be the change you wish to see in the world.**" And so I have. THE FIGHTING SOUL does not make many friends as we force people to look at their real values, their double standards and their actions. **We do walk our talk.** We care deeply about justice, people's struggles and the survival of our planet. We are a voice for fairness - for seniors, for children, for animals, and for plants. We work to bring hope to the forgotten. I am one of those fighting souls.

"Life is not a matter of holding good cards, but of playing a poor hand well."
Robert Louis Stevenson

1 - Six Walks to Heaven

1998 - Valentine's Weekend - Flat-lined Seven Times

I was in a loveless marriage. I had grown up in a home with abuse; a verbally, physically, and sexually abusive father who abandoned us many times. I had no role models for healthy, caring relationships or for respect. I was always afraid and always worried about the next things that would go wrong, be blamed on me, and cause me to be tortured again.

Some of my memories are too horrific to write about or even to focus on recalling. My mother was weak and sick. She never protected me. As the oldest of four, everything fell upon my shoulders. At age 17, I graduated from high school in Indianapolis, Indiana. I took a Grey Hound bus to Bloomington, Indiana, and set about securing an apartment for my family and to find work. I, also, had to go before a Board of old men to secure National Defense Loans. Since I didn't have any parental homebase, I had no financial records to use to apply for any scholarships. I was able to quickly find three part-time jobs that would allow me to attend classes at Indiana University during the day. I found jobs at the Art Library, at Montgomery Wards catalog center, and at one of the dorms helping with the lunch service. I started work and found an apartment. Soon, I was also in class. I made friends with the two older ladies who ran the Art Library and eventually became brave enough to ask a great favor of them. Would they take me to Indianapolis to get two of my younger siblings out of an orphanage to bring them back to Bloomington, Indiana - about 102 miles. These kind ladies did so.

They took me to Indianapolis and without an appointment, in 1964, I took my two youngest siblings - Mary Alice, 11, and Chuck, 7, out of an orphanage to help raise while I worked my way through college. I was 17. However, apparently, having the two older ladies with me, I think the orphanage officials assumed that they would be caring for Mary Alice and Chuck.

Life has always been difficult for me, especially since I am shy. I share this with you so that you can know that I am not a special person. I am an ordinary person with great trials and tribulations to overcome. I have been a strong advocate for children and our environment most of my life. I saw that education would be my only way out of poverty.

I have always been highly allergic and sickly. As an adult, I often dealt with infections, especially sinus infections. In 1998 I was on an antibiotic - that I had taken before - for a sinus infection. However, this time something was terribly wrong. I could tell that I was having a reaction to the antibiotic I was taking. It was Sunday morning. Larry, my husband, had taken Jonathan, our son, to Church. I took liquid and pill forms of Benadryl. And, I flushed my body with baking soda water. An acid system has greater allergic reactions. None of these calmed my symptoms. I was hot, red, and broken out in hives all over. I dressed and drove myself to the hospital, about 10 minutes away. When I checked into the emergency room, I handed them my prescription bottle, told them what was happening, and how I had treated myself. They immediately took me back. This was my second clue that I was in trouble, no forms and no waiting room for me. I was having a severe allergic reaction to the antibiotic. **I WENT INTO ANAPHYLACTIC SHOCK** soon after arriving at Good Sam Hospital, in the western suburbs of Chicago. **I FLAT-LINED 7 TIMES !!!**

*The first time I flat-lined was the most memorable as I peacefully left my body and walked a lighted path towards Jesus. He had a simple robe belted with a rope. Jesus' hair was dark brown, almost black, and shoulder length; his skin was brown, and he had a beard.

Twice, during this first walk, I stopped to question God about not being ready to die. I worried about my messy basement and about who would raise Jonathan. However, **walking the light was so peaceful, pain-free, and joyful, that I let go of my concerns and lived in the warmth of the blissful light as a spirit**. I perceived everything around me. The medical room seemed to have grown taller as I walked to heaven. I could see the desperate work to bring me back to life under me, while feeling calm and peaceful; idyllic as I walked the light. Below me, the medical staff frantically worked attempting to resuscitate my body. My soul walked the light and I had never known such calm and peace. There was no fear. Below me, my body was not breathing and I didn't have a heartbeat. Above, I walked to Jesus and touched his out-stretched hand, I knew that was the exact moment of death as I could see how frantically below me the medical team worked to bring me back. The head female doctor lifted my upper body off the gurney, yelled at me several times about staying with them, and was slapping me across the face numerous times. I kept hearing, **"Diane, stay with us !"** I wanted to stay with Jesus.

I asked Jesus about **EVIL**. We did not speak, but exchanged thoughts. We walked in a field of yellow light. Jesus explained that God had given people the gift of **FREE WILL**. Many did not make good choices. As I walked with Jesus, I asked more about **EVIL**. He **explained that it is God's gift of FREE WILL that allowed humans to decide for themselves how they will use this gift.** Some people will make the world better and some selfish people will think about themselves only and share little. Jesus explained why speaking the **TRUTH** was so important. Being **HONEST** helps humans use their gift of FREE WILL well. Dishonest people will use their FREE WILL to manipulate and control others. Jesus spoke about self-centered, selfish people who use other people. Below me, because of their heroic efforts, I was soon back in my body; but, only conscious for moments. I wanted to tell the head doctor to stop slapping me and I wanted to tell the medical team to let me go. However, I faded into unconsciousness again. Soon, I was walking the path of light again towards Jesus. My Spirit walked to Heaven while my body and my brain were turned off below in my lifeless body as I flat-lined in the hospital. The only moments I have felt really loved, at peace, and safe were the moments I spent in Heaven.

In walking with Jesus the second time, I was told that we have **two purposes in life - to take care of each other and **to take care of our planet and the creatures who share our world**. We are all supposed to be stewards of our planet, the animals, and the plants. Jesus told me that this is where FREE WILL is so important. He explained how greediness could ravage the wonders of the world and make Earth uninhabitable for plants, animals, and eventually humans. He reminded me about how children needed honest people to care of their planet until they inherited it. Jesus said that materialistic people will try to use the blessings of the Earth to enrich themselves. He warned me that wealthy people can be dangerous in their need and greed to gather more wealth.

No words were ever spoken; we exchanged thoughts, Jesus and I. Again, I was pulled back into my body and back into the human world. I didn't want to be there. I wanted to stay in the light and warmth of Heaven with Jesus. Each time that I was aware of being back in my body, the head doctor had lifted my upper body off the gurney. I would be conscious and aware of her yelling at me and slapping me; then, I would fade into unconsciousness again. I was hooked up to all kinds of machines and surrounded by medical staff. No one worked as hard to save me as the female doctor. She was a fighting soul trying to save my life. Nevertheless, I kept being pulled back to Heaven.

*** On my third walk, **I was told how much God values diversity**. Jesus said that a person can't love GOD and be a racist. God created diversity in all things - people, animals, and plants. All have value and purpose. **Jesus explained how all humans have black roots;** and therefore, no race is more important than another race. He mentioned his own brown skin and that the Bible is about people with brown skin. Again, Jesus warned me that some folks will see the color of their skin as a passport to entitlement. This was not God's plan. Jesus said that God wants diversity in all things to thrive. God wants people with different abilities, different sexual orientations, and different skin color to all be welcomed into the Kingdom of Heaven. Jesus told me to continue to stand up for humans with differences. He told me that a human variance will not keep a person from Heaven; however, **discrimination will**. I felt comfort in knowing that in the human world I had been making good choices in spite of my hardships. I felt peaceful and purposeful. I was comfortable with Jesus. I wanted to stay in the bliss of Heaven. However, I was again pulled back into my human experience. I was being slapped and yelled at. I tried to talk; but then I was unconscious again.

****On my fourth walk with Jesus, I was told that real Christians follow him - **feed the hungry, shelter the homeless, and care for the sick**. Jesus warned me about **False Christians** and **Double Standards**. He reminded me of the saying, *"Actions speak louder than words".* Jesus counseled me about evil people who claim to be good, but aren't. He told me to watch people's actions more than listening to their words. He reminded me that people with FREE WILL can say anything. He suggested that I focus on people's actions and ask myself if they care about others and if they care about God's creations or is their real focus themselves. Jesus said that REAL Christians are humble and don't demand attention; they go about God's work in quiet ways. REAL Christians care about others and reach out to take care of others. REAL Christians aren't drawing attention to themselves. They acknowledge their blessings with **GRATITUDE** and share with others quietly. Fake Christians support injustice, inequality, control over others, entitlement, greed and war. Jesus told me that bad choices do have consequences. He said that Fake Christians will not walk in the Light. Jesus said that I could learn from the words of wise, old souls. I soaked in all of these teachings. I no longer cared if I stayed in Heaven or if I returned to Earth. God would decide. I especially tried to remember Jesus' warnings. I loved the bright warmth of Heaven. I felt so calm and relaxed. We walked and talked like friends; Jesus and I. ..... Again, I was startled by being slapped and by being yelled at. My thought was, I am back in my body again. I tried to say,

"Stop slapping me !" But it went dark and quiet again.

"Those who can make you believe absurdities; can make you commit atrocities." Voltaire

*****The next time, Jesus talked about **Earth**, the plants and creatures we share the planet with. I love the wonders of earth, big and small. However, Jesus was saddened by the ways that humans had allowed greed to destroy the beauty and the variety of Earth. I told Jesus that I never tired of seeing beauty in the world, even little insects. Jesus said that God had given us such luxury with great variety. We have not appreciated our gifts nor have we taken care of them. In fact, we had killed large animals just for trophies. This is so sorrowful to his father - GOD. Jesus said that extreme

12

WEATHER, caused by human FREE WILL, will show humans the error of their ways. Jesus warned me that many will suffer and die while learning this lesson. Earth's plants and animals will also suffer and die. Jesus said that the Earth has too many selfish people who don't want to care and to share - too many people who only want to do things their way without consideration of others or of consequences. Earth has too many people focused on gathering wealth and fame. Sadly, so many plants and animals are disappearing. Jesus said that there are also too many people on Earth for the planet to support life well. He said that FREE WILL is allowing greed to kill many things without noticing the consequences. I felt sad as I walked with Jesus this time. I felt sad to be part of the human race that was so destructive. I felt sorrowful that people were not paying attentions to the warnings they had been given. I felt sad that human greed was so destructive. I wanted to say, *"Stop shaking me !"* I was being slapped and yelled at again. This doctor would not give up on me. She was a fighting soul. Then, it was dark and quiet once more.

******My sixth walk with Jesus was personal; I was told that I was to **live in JOY** and that I needed to end my bad marriage. Larry, my husband, and his family would never appreciate me and they would forever want me to become Catholic. This was not my purpose. Jesus told me that belonging to a certain religion would never get people into Heaven; nor would going to church every week; nor would reading the Bible daily. He told me that the way a person lives is what is important. Do they care about others and do they take care of the world ? Jesus said that I was to use my gifts in art and as a passionate environmentalist. I was to continue to always **speak the truth**. Jesus warned me, like him, many will not like me because the truth reflects other people's dishonesty and greed. He told me that, like him, I will often find myself alone, because humans want control more than they want truth. Jesus reminded me of how difficult he found getting humans to change their ways. People in power want to maintain their control, at any cost.

Jesus told me that my journey of honesty and warning would be difficult. He cautioned me that Fake Christians would be the most difficult people to deal with as they think quoting Bible verses is important; however, walking the way of the Bible is the way to Heaven. Jesus told me to continue my deep concern for feeding the poor and for caring about children. He told me that even though I am humble, I needed to speak up for children, their planet, and the truth. Jesus told me that I was to be an example of a REAL CHRISTIAN who walked her talk - someone whose actions mirrored her words. I knew with these teachings that I was going to return to earth and to continue my human experience. Jesus was giving me directions to live by.

God decided that I should stay on earth, so I did live.

On the way to the ICU, two attending nurses questioned me about my experience. I told them that I knew that I died, walked the light to Heaven, talked with Jesus, and came back numerous times. I told the nurses that I knew that the head female doctor kept lifting my upper body off the gurney, she kept yelling at me, she kept shaking me, and she kept slapping me. They were surprised that I knew this. The nurses told me that I had made medical history at the hospital because I had flat-lined seven times and lived.

"You are a Medical Miracle," they exclaimed !!!

God decided that I should stay, was my answer. I **wanted to stay in the light, peace, and joy of Heaven. It was so wonderful to be in Heaven.**

Afterwards, I was stable, but had to spend three days in the ICU for observation and to make sure the antibiotic was out of my system. Initially, my experiences were recorded to be added to my medical records. Then, many medical folks came to talk to me about my near-death experience out of curiosity. I shared and in return, they shared other experiences that they had been told by patients in the hospital. Apparently, **not everyone's death experience is peaceful and joyful**. Several nurses retold stories that they had heard from their patients about dying and being chased by black wispy spirits into darkness. These experiences were described as terrifying and apparently meant to serve as a warning. According to these nurses, these patients totally changed their lives around to be more positive, more caring, and more generous.

From my experience, I did divorce Larry in 1999. And, I have had angels with me daily ever since. As I have aged past 75, I am very aware of how many times angels catch me and prevent a bad fall. My days are filled with **words of gratitude** for my angel's help and with words of **requests for safety and protection and comfort**, for myself and for others. I so often pray for the world to be safe for all children. I guess because I always have angels with me is why I haven't had any more recent encounters. I am embraced by angels daily. My experience of flat-lining seven times and living to talk about my experience is part of the Good Sam Hospital's medical records - in Downers Grove, Illinois in the western suburbs of Chicago. I do see the world very differently than most. I am very intuitive about fakes, lies, and manipulation maneuvers. I am sadly aware of how self-centered and ungrateful most humans are. Jesus told me that people who complain constantly are not grateful for their blessings. This is so discouraging. And, I am sad to see so many plants and animals vanishing. I have deep sorrow about the dying planet that we are leaving the next generations. I am aware of young and older souls quickly. Jesus was right, people don't want to hear that they are fake Christians and they don't want to change. Young souls are especially egotistical and consuming. They aren't easy to be around, as they fill a space with their noise.

When I think back to this experience, it is a reminder that we are not alone on our journeys on Earth, even when we may feel abandoned by other humans. I left my body six times while unconscious on a hospital gurney. My experience just confirmed my values, beliefs, and purposes. People should always come before money, power and greed. Plus, I learned firsthand that we are more than our physical bodies. Our **SOULS ARE ETERNAL. I AM ETERNAL; YOU ARE ETERNAL.**

The only question is, do you want to make your eternal experience, blissful or terrifying ???

Two months after this near-death experience, I attended an art exhibit of famous Chicago Fires. The paintings were large and the details in each were remarkable. One could see the bricks and the window sills of the tall buildings. Items through the windows shown. The people on the streets were tiny, but painted with incredible details. As I went from painting to painting, I was stunned. It was clear to me that this artist had endured a near-death experience. He had painted people laying on stretchers, laying on sidewalks, and laying on gurneys with souls emerging from them. Viewing these painting sent a chill of remembrance through my body.

WE ARE ALL ETERNAL !

"My sheep hear my voice, and I know them, and they follow me: and I give unto them eternal life; and they shall never perish." Bible: John 10:27-2

2 - First Angel Encounter
1974 - before cell phones

"The wings of angels are hope and faith."
Omar M Al-aqeel

"An angel of God never has wings." Joseph Smith, Jr.

In the fall of 1974, I was traveling to DeKalb, Illinois from the Chicago area after school to work on my Master's Degree in Elementary Education with an Art minor. At this time there were no cell phones and the road to DeKalb was a two-lane country road bordered on both sides by cornfields. One dark foggy night, about 10:00 p.m., while driving home from an Art Class, I had a problem with my car wobbling. I pulled over onto the narrow gravel shoulder. I said a quick prayer, *Angels please help me*. I got out of my car to check my tires. All of a sudden, without a sound, two lights - like headlights, and a man appeared.

"Flat tire?" he asked.
"Yes, it looks like it," I stammered. "I have never changed a tire before," I added.
"Is there a spare in the trunk?" he questioned.
"Yes, I think so".
We took my art materials from my trunk, laid them on the ground, and uncovered the spare tire and the jack. I couldn't see much because of the glare of the two headlights behind my car and because of the man's hat. The quiet man with the hat changed my flat tire without conversation. However, he couldn't get my hub cap back on.
This is when I said, **"Oh, I am just coming from an Art class and I have a hammer in my class tools."** I pulled a hammer from my art supplies (*thinking, this is when he kills me*). He taped the hub cap back on. I put the hammer back in my trunk and before I could

turn around, the lights and the man were gone. No car had passed me. The man and the lights just disappeared. No traffic had passed from either direction. I just stood looking out into the darkness for a few seconds in disbelief. Where had he gone? How had he appeared and now disappeared so quickly? Was there another car? How had the other car disappeared without a sound? I didn't imagine the man. Someone changed my tire. And, I didn't get to even properly thank him. Who changed my tire? It took me years of replaying this scenario in my head to realize that I had been helped/blessed by an angel that night. I couldn't wrap my thinking around such an unimportant person as myself being helped by an angel - maybe even my guardian angel.

When one has an open, grateful heart, amazing things can happen.

"All God's angels come to us disguised." James Russell Lowell

"Being an angel to someone gives you the chance to leave a wonderful legacy." Angel quotes.

In the Bible there are many angels appearing. In the Old Testament, angels were present at creation; when Hagar conceived Abraham's child; three angels visited Abraham; two angels rescued Lot from destruction of Sodom; Jacob had several angel encounters, most noted is his famous dream; the angel of death & the Passover angel; angels present at the giving of the law; in Stephen's speech angels were present at the giving of the law; an angel was sent to warn Balaam that he has disobeyed God; an angel was used to rebuke Israel for their idolatry; an angel cursed enemies of God during the time of the Judges; angels judged Israel for David's

18

sin; an angel brought Elijah food and drink to strengthen him; angels killed many of the Assyrians army; angels save Hananiah, Mishael, and Azariah from the fiery furnace; and an angel saved Daniel from the lion's den. These are just the angels of the Old Testament. God has used angels regularly.

https://www.blueletterbible.org/faq/don_stewart/don_stewart_19.cfm

In the New Testament, angels appeared to Zacharias in Jerusalem's temple; Gabriel was sent to Mary to inform her of her conception; Joseph received three separate angels visits; an angel announced Jesus' birth; angels ministered to Jesus after his temptation by Satan; God sent an angel to Jesus before his death; two angels appeared to the disciples on Mount of Olives right after Jesus' ascension into Heaven; God sent an angel to free the twelve apostles from prison; an angel told Philip to travel to Gaza; an angel was sent to Cornelius to seek out Peter; an angel appeared to Paul and told him he and all on the ship would be saved; an angel visited John and revealed prophecies that become the book of Revelation; and John has four other angels visit when he is hungry, when he is told to measure God's temple, when he is told about a woman riding a scarlet beast, and when he is told that the prophecies he saw will come to pass and that he is to worship God.

https://www.biblestudy.org/question/angels-in-new-testament.html

I have no idea why a humble soul, like me, was blessed with the help from an angel; however, I am most grateful. People do seem to be more open to talking about angel encounters these days.

3 - Abusive Father; Weak Mother
RA since I was 8 years old

"It is during the worst times of your life that you will get to see the true colors of the people who say they care for you." Anonymous

Even if you are an introvert with a physical and a sexually abusive background like me, you are not alone. I was born 11 months after my parents married. My brother, Johnny, was born 13 months after me. Soon, there were four of us. This was difficult for my father who had always been a self-centered only child adored by his parents and two aunts who had no children of their own. Even later with four children, my father always put himself first. He ate well when sometimes we had nothing to eat. My father abandoned us regularly. As was my father's life pattern; whenever something happened that he didn't like, it was always someone else's fault. As the oldest child, who worked to be perfect, it was usually my fault. As the scapegoat, I was regularly battered and even sexually assaulted. In those days, no one ever asked about my bruises. I was raised in the Air Force so we moved every year or two.

Usually, we moved every year as my father's superiors tried to help hide his alcoholism. Being shy, I never had friends and I never talked to anyone about the horrors of my home life. I often cried silently inside. No one would have comforted me had I verbalized my tears. There were no child advocates in those days, and fathers had supreme power and control.

"I cannot think of any need in childhood as strong as the need for a father's protection." Sigmund Freud.

20

To this day I have sleep issues. As a child I was conditioned to believe that if I went to sleep, I would be hurt or bad things would happen to me. This fear has followed me through life. I am sure that other abused children, who are lucky enough to grow up, have this same kind of issue resulting from their childhood traumas.

Being raised Southern Baptist by my Mississippi born and raised mother, I would always wonder, **"Where is God ?"** I sometimes found some comfort hiding in a closet crying out loud. If my father had heard me, he would have beaten me more. My father said that my abuse was always my fault and I grew up believing if I could just be perfect enough, I wouldn't be abused by men. I often thought about killing my father or killing myself. I wondered if I was strong enough to kill him without him cutting off my arm first.

By the age of eight (1954), my fingers had started to curl and I was diagnosed with RA = Rheumatoid Arthritis. My abuse was beginning to manifest itself internally as well as externally. My fingers were taped on boards nightly to prevent my hand from becoming knots. Later, doctors would connect the dots and tell me that my childhood RA had been triggered by the traumas of my regular abuse. Neither my mother or my siblings ever tried to stop my father. They were all terrified of him as well. He was a man without a heart - a dark, young soul. I always prayed to be adopted.

I am 75 years old now and I was regularly sexually abused by my father as a child. No one talked about it in those days. I was lean and often hungry. Neither of my parents ever hugged or kissed me. I do remember my mother being affectionate towards my two younger siblings, Mary Alice and Chuck. Me - I had come along and ended the blissfulness of their first year of marriage. Plus, at birth I was severely allergic. I couldn't keep Mother's milk or formula down. Goat's milk saved my life. I often wondered why God had led the doctors to goat's milk and saved me. Many times, I would think it would have been better had I died shortly after birth.

As the oldest of four, I had to raise myself and my siblings. I never got to be loved or valued as a child. I never was a child or even a teenager. I was just the unappreciated worker. I was always just a dependable kid saddled with adult responsibilities and burdens. My being was about trying to hold a very dysfunctional family together. The harder I tried, the more I failed. My father took everything and never loved any of the five of us. My mother was a weak young soul as well. She wasn't strong enough to protect us.

As I aged, my RA ravaged my joints, especially my knee joints. At age 75, I have had 16 surgeries and procedures on my knees. I have been walking with the aid of a cane since 2017. Every day, I give thanks for the mobility that I do have; and, my SIGHT. People all over the world, with my rare eye condition, are blind. And, some with RA are on walkers or in wheelchairs. I work daily and nightly to keep my fingers straightened. I am blessed.

Life has taught me that most people want to be heard, but they do not want to listen. And, they truly do not want to listen to me talk about my pain; physical or emotional. People have their own pain. So, my pains are my constant companions; and, we are silent. **I try to overcome this profound loneliness with gratitude.**

"Gratitude is not only the greatest of virtues, but the parent of all others." Marcus Tullius Cicero

4 - Blue-winged Monarch

I have always seen myself as a blue-winged Monarch - someone with gifts and talents; yet, never belonging. I have always been a people-pleaser and a humble servant. I was the one who always flew in to clean up the messes of my family. Others have occupied the spotlight in my life. I have written my story many times to myself.

Many years ago, a blue-winged Monarch emerged from a chrysalis hanging from a milkweed plant. Once emerged, the Monarch was so excited about the wonderful metamorphosis that had taken place. She stretched out her new wings in delight; welcoming the drying warmth of the sun. Then, with great exuberance, she tested her new wings - awkwardly at first, but then with feather-weight grace. She felt so proud of her new body, her new wings, and her new abilities.

However, in only a few days, the blue-winged Monarch realized that she was very different. It was difficult being blue-winged. At first, she hadn't realized how different she was, nor how other Monarchs would react towards her. She really did love her blue wings, so she tried to believe that God had made her extraordinarily special for a remarkable purpose. Still, the other Monarchs wanted her to conform to look and be like them. So, the blue-winged Monarch tried. She tried numerous ways to conceal her blue wings so that she could be more like the others. She wanted to relate to the other Monarchs. Unfortunately, she did not have orange wings. She did not belong to the Monarch group.

In fact, the other Monarchs saw her as unsightly. They even tried to change her so that she would fit in. Her few friends and her elders were always giving her advice about how she could change herself to be more like the orange-winged Monarchs. The blue-winged Monarch loved her uniqueness. She tried to hide her sadness with her search for her special purpose. However, she was a misfit. The other Monarchs wanted her to have orange wings just like theirs. The blue-winged Monarch really did like her blue wings. However, out of loneliness, she tried to change herself -- she tried to conform. Once she even had a brilliant red cardinal sprinkle her wings with pollen to cover the cobalt blue color. The wind blew the pollen away. Even with all of her efforts to become more like the others, she wasn't.

The blue-winged Monarch became increasingly dissatisfied with herself and with others trying to change her. She started avoiding the other Monarchs, even hiding so that she would not be told that she needed to change. Her loneliness and isolation grew. She often wondered why God had not made her like all the other orange-winged Monarchs. It was lonely being unique. She longed to feel connected and accepted. Yet, it just seemed, when she was delighted in being who she was, others were quick to remind her of how she should be. Other Monarchs wanted her to be just like them.

As time passed it became more difficult for the blue-winged Monarch to smile or to sail through the air. She even gave up trying to have the strength and the courage to embrace her life, just as it was.

The blue-winged Monarch had so enjoyed giving to others. She was careful to compliment and to lift others up. She tried to be a friend to herself and to other creatures. The blue-winged Monarch tried to understand others and to be accepting of them, even when they did not accept her. She tried not to focus on seeking approval. The blue-winged Monarch wanted to be accepting of herself and to find joy in her uniqueness. She even tried to overcome her loneliness and her isolation.

As time passed, the blue-winged Monarch became discouraged. It was hard to like yourself when all those around you wanted you to change.

The days grew shorter and the nights grew cooler. An elder orange-winged Monarch announced that it was time to prepare for the journey south --- the migration to Mexico. The blue-winged Monarch was very excited about this news. She loved adventures. Her mind raced with thoughts of the fun it would be, traveling as a group to the mountain forests near Mexico City. She had never been out of her own meadow before. Oh, how she loved events. They were like celebrations.

The blue-winged Monarch wondered how they would make this trip. She wondered why they were taking this fantastic journey. She even wondered how far thousands of miles were ? What is winter, that they were searching refuge from ? What would it be like to fly over forest, mountains, water, and even deserts to get to Mexico ? **WOW ! What an adventure !**

She didn't understand the concern of the older adult Monarchs when they worried if there would be enough fir trees left in the highland winter home or if logging had taken many more down. What did fir trees look like anyway ?

The days grew even shorter and the nights colder; so, grew the excitement surrounding the winter migration. The Monarchs waited for their friends and cousins to arrive from Canada and the eastern United States. The blue-winged Monarch wondered if they would find enough nectar from the goldenrod and the asters along the way to eat. This would be a remarkable trip. How did the elders know which way to fly, she wondered.

As Monarchs from the north arrived, some vegetation became covered with clusters of orange and black Monarchs. They really are beautiful thought the blue-winged Monarch. She was so excited about this building adventure. For a while, she almost forgot about her own problem.

Unfortunately, the newly arriving Monarchs had never seen a blue-winged Monarch before. They taunted, teased, and had more suggestions about how she could change to be more like them. They even told her that if she did not become an orange-winged Monarch, she could never make a successful migration.

The blue-winged Monarch sadly flew away, to be by herself. Maybe she should just stay behind. The trip would be difficult enough without feeling as though you were not connected to the group. She didn't know what to do.

After days of agonizing thoughts, the blue-winged Monarch made her decision. It wouldn't be easy; however, in her heart she had decided that it would be best to be true to herself. Maybe, she would even find another blue-winged Monarch.

Loneliness is one of the greatest pains.

I would like to inspire others who feel like me, like they are blue-winged Monarchs, to feel valued and to know that God has a plan for you also. Your own beautiful caring character is more important than being part of a group or a cult.

This is the lesson I still have to learn.

"Butterflies cannot see their wings, but the rest of the world can. You are beautiful and while you may not see it, we can." Naya Rivera

5 - Africa and Childhood
16 Schools, Summers in Mississippi, & Siblings

My father was in the Air Force and because of his intelligence and his alcoholism, we moved every year. We lived in four different countries in Africa: French Morocco, Morocco, Algeria, and Libya. My experiences in Africa were eye-opening - being a white minority, seeing so many more dress codes, and participating in so many different cultural practices. Traveling to and from Africa with the Air Force was not luxury - people were like cargo. In fact, we traveled to Africa in a cargo plane.

C-124 plane for crossing the Atlantic. January 1952, this was our family's ride to Rabat, Morocco in Africa.

"The aircraft capable of transporting 200 troops and their gear, along with fully assembled tanks, field guns and trucks was a marvel on the tarmac due to its clamshell doors that split wide open under the nose to load cargo by a hydraulic ramp."

"The Douglas **C-124** Globemaster II, nicknamed "Old Shaky", is an American heavy-lift cargo aircraft built by the Douglas Aircraft." "It was also really noisy, and would creak and groan a lot," There was no toilet; just several chamber pots. The Air Force also, called it the "FLYING Box Car". https://www.airplanes-online.com/c124-globemaster.htm

3,626 miles - **January 1952** - This distance is from New York City, New York - USA to Rabat, Morocco - Africa. The 12 hour flight with in-flight refueling. "In-flight Refueling Specialists pump thousands of gallons of jet fuel into aircraft in need of fuel". C-124 traveled about 300 miles an hour. Seats pulled down from the sides of the plane. Cargo road in the middle. To this day, I can remember the horrific noise. I was sure the plane would fall apart before we reached land again. Johnny and I were terrified into stillness.

I am the girl standing on the right - the oldest. I had just turned 5 years old. Johnny is 4, Mary Alice is 6 months.

This is what we ate.

"**C-Rations** were developed in 1938 as a replacement for reserve rations, which sustained troops during World War I, and consisted chiefly of canned corned beef or bacon and cans of hardtack biscuits, as well as ground coffee, sugar, salt and tobacco with rolling paper, & hard chocolate. "

Our return to the United States - New York was on June 1955 on this ship.

"The USNS Private William H. Thomas was a **Tryon-class evacuation transport built in 1941 that was renamed in 1946 for a Wynne (Cross County) native who received a Medal of Honor during World War II**. The 7,100-ton vessel was 450 feet long and sixty-two feet wide, reaching speeds of eighteen knots. Crewed by **forty officers and 409 enlisted men**, the Rixey had hospital wards for sixty-two officers and 1,221 enlisted men. It was decommissioned on March 27, 1946, having earned four battle stars during the war."

"After the Japanese attacked Pearl Harbor on December 7, 1941, the U.S. Navy requisitioned the ship and commissioned it as USS *Rixey* (APH-3), a **casualty evacuation ship**, on December 30, 1941." https://www.maritime.dot.gov/history/gallant-ship-award/usns-pvt-william-h-thomas

When we returned from Africa, we moved to Midwest City, Oklahoma. Chuck was born.

We all have a great connection to Africa. A decade-long DNA project, 2005-2015, by National Geographic collected DNA samples from individuals all over the planet. It was the largest and most intensive DNA project ever conducted on the planet and resulted in a startling discovery; **every living person on Earth is a direct descendant of one woman who lived in East Africa 150,000 years ago**. They named her "**Mitochondrial Eve**".

I know about this study because I participated in it and donated my own DNA in 2010. **We all have black roots.** Unfortunately, the study was shut down because some folks didn't like the results - didn't like having black roots. DNA was collected in this study from more than 997,222 people from 140 countries around the world. https://cruwys.blogspot.com/2019/06/the-end-of-public-participation-in.html
Rupert Murdoch bought out the media arm of National Geographic and ended its not-for-profit status, and this study.

Africa is believed to be the **cradle of humans**. For me, as a child, it was a shocking and new awareness of dark-skinned people; women covered and veiled except for their eyes; streets filled with different smells and sounds; and people who spoke languages that I didn't understand. Africa made me aware of God's purposeful diversity. As a child, every place I saw new wonders and different architecture and dissimilar customs. I was always in awe of the variety and also fearful at the same time by all of the fascinating differences. While in Africa, we always lived off base, so we were very aware of the African ways. To this day, I can remember how loud the streets became at night during Islamic holidays. Once when my brother, Johnny, and I were in a local park by ourselves, I fell into a pond while we were walking around the cement edges. I can still remember falling and falling and falling. I never touched the bottom. A kind Arabic man pulled me out of the well. Another time, I remember the great drama when a little American girl, my age, was kidnapped by an Arabic man on a bicycle. As a child, everything in Africa was big and strange and dramatic.

Africa opened my eyes and my heart to diversity and variety. It was clear to me that whites weren't the chosen people of God. It was no longer races, but **the Human Race** in my mind.

"**The Presbyterian Church seminars have been teaching that Jesus had brown/dark skin and that the Bible is about brown/dark skinned people since the 1960s.**"
Rev. David Nash

One time our family of five was traveling from one African country to another in a small Renault car. We came upon a place where the road had ended. The road and the village had been swallowed up by a recent earthquake. I remember standing on the dry dirt and trying to imagine how the big crack had opened up and swallowed up an entire village; huts, people, and animals. This was the first time that I had seen the destructive force of Nature. I was astounded.

I remember group desert trips and group trips to the Mediterranean Sea. I have ridden a camel in the desert. The camels crossing a desert were amazing. I saw camels in cities as well. I have traveled to see magnificent wildlife. I have seen large animals killed by natives for food. I was very impressed by large animals. What I don't understand is wildlife being killed for fun as trophies. I was shocked to see men with guns shoot wildlife for sport. I was speechless. I have never forgotten the first blood flow from a large animal shot for game. How heartless of humans.

Africa - is the scene of horrific injustices towards large wildlife by **Trophy Hunters**. I will never understand how any human could kill a magnificent animal for amusement. I am sure that this doesn't please God either. "Trophy hunters pay huge sums of money to kill wild animals for in-home display. They enter their achievements into record books kept by member organizations. Trophy hunting harms conservation by exacerbating the population decline of many imperiled species. Compared to trophy hunting, wildlife-watching tourism generates far more income to support conservation and provides far more jobs to local people." https://www.hsi.org/issues/trophy-hunting/ **345 Trophy animals enter the US daily.** The United States is the #1 importer. **200,000 threatened or endangered animals are killed for trophies each year.** "Killing the strongest male of an animal species results in scores of additional deaths. For examples, when a dominant African lion is killed, females and cubs are vulnerable to hostile pride takeover by another male, who will kill the previous lion's cubs." "The most coveted animals for trophies are elephants, lions, rhinos and leopards." I wonder how hell will feel for these trophy hunters without protection when they are being chased by these wild animals ? **Real Christians would be animal defenders.**

"It's not whether animals will survive, it's whether man has the will to save them." Anthony Douglas Williams

My father's alcoholism kept us moving in the Air Force, a new country or a new state every year. I went to 16 schools before I graduated from high school. Being the new kid every year in a new school and being very shy and introverted always left me open to being bullied. Plus, I often had bruises. And my childhood rheumatoid arthritis in my hands, feet and knees made childhood activities and actions difficult for me. My joints were stiff and my hands were curling. My clothes were often homemade or second hand. I was drab, scared, skittish and lonely. I never said anything in class. I was and wanted to be invisible.

My one break from my father's abuse was getting to spend three summers in Mississippi in my grandmother's shack on a cotton farm. I was small and it wasn't easy picking cotton in the sweltering summer heat; however, I knew even when my skin shed in sheets from sunburns; at least, I would have food to eat and I wouldn't be assaulted. Plus, I think my grandmother really cared about me. I was so afraid all the time that I never shared with her what my life was like being battered and sexually abused regularly. I had come to believe it was my fault and I didn't want anyone to know. I was ashamed. I never saw any adult as an advocate for me. I just quietly did whatever I was told to do day after day and cried on the inside. My cotton-picking partners were blacks. I witnessed firsthand how difficult their life was and how hard survival was. I walked in their shoes.

I was the oldest of four children born to totally dysfunctional parents. My father was selfish and self-absorbed, and didn't want children. He never wanted to share anything and he felt like the world owed him. He had been raised as an indulged, spoiled only child. My mother was a weak woman who wanted children to adore her. She had several health issues and was not able to care for children well. I always remember her napping every afternoon. Responsibilities fell to me early.

At age eight, I was cooking and cleaning and washing clothes in a sink and drying socks on an oven rack with the oven on and the door open to heat the room. I never went out to play, but it didn't matter because my hands had started to curl and my knees had stiffened so I couldn't do things that other children could do. My knees and fingers hurt constantly and I couldn't run well or ride a bike. I never owned a bike. When I was outside, I was taking care of my siblings.

"The hard times that you go through build character, making you A MUCH STRONGER PERSON." Rita Mero

I even took my siblings to college with me. Without a car, we walked everywhere. The outcome of this story is that I did graduate from Indiana University with a teaching degree and years of National Defense loans. And, to this day, Mary Alice and Chuck have nothing to do with me. They say that I was too controlling and too bossy. I wish they could have walked in my shoes. It wasn't my job to raise them while growing up or while working my way through college. Since I was the person who kept stepping up to try to hold the family together, they feel that I am to blame for all of our family dysfunction. This is one of those times in life that I kept asking myself, what would Jesus do - and I did it. Unfortunately, like Jesus, I was not and am not appreciated.

"Courage doesn't always roar. Sometimes courage is the quiet voice at the end of the day saying "I will try again tomorrow." " Mary Anne Radmacher

In the meantime, my brother Johnny, was trying to graduate from high school, living with a friend. Johnny graduated and then started college part-time while working his way through. Unfortunately, he was drafted for Viet Nam. The poor young men go first. Luckily, Johnny survived.

"The human capacity for burden is like bamboo – far more flexible than you'd ever believe at first glance."
Jodi Picoult

6 - Second Angel Encounter
Fibromyalgia

Yes, I Do Know How Tired You Are and How Much You Hurt. Fibromyalgia, 1982

Every day I wake up to an alarm clock, even on weekends. *Please, God, can't I stay in bed, a bit longer ?* It is 6:00 a.m. My night was restless, as always awakened by pain, by sleep apnea, and by a trip to the bathroom. In bed, I stretch and bend, trying to wake up my tired muscles and stiff joints. I am in a constant state of chronic pain and exhaustion. I remind myself to say, *Good Day, God !* instead of *Good God, DAY !.* I adjust my attitude, get out of bed and try to stand up straight, and smile. My movements are slow as I make my way to the bathroom. Warm water, actually HOT water, is always a blessing. I keep reminding myself - *Make an EFFORT - not an excuse.* I picture Jesus carrying the cross and remind myself that my cross is not nearly as heavy. **Hopeful determination is helpful.** I have Fibromyalgia. I live with constant pain in my joints and in my muscles. Little was known about this condition in 1982. Still, **gratitude and purpose served me well**.

I make my way downstairs - my knees hurt so badly that I stop after every few steps and take a break. I am 36. My right knee burns and feels like it is being squeezed in a vice. I wish I could go back to bed. I tell myself to stop whining and to be grateful that I have feet and knees to move me, and that I have a wonderful job to go to. I love being a teacher. In 1980, my doctors wanted to put me on disability. Through much medical trial and error and my own true grit, I am still functioning today at age 75. *"Fibromyalgia is a disorder characterized by widespread musculoskeletal pain accompanied by fatigue, sleep, memory and mood issues."*

"Fibromyalgia amplifies painful sensations by affecting the way your brain and spinal cord process painful and nonpainful signals."
https://www.cdc.gov/arthritis/basics/fibromyalgia.htm#:~:text=q uality%20of%20life%3F-,What%20is%

Fibro consumes one's entire body. In my case, my Fibromyalgia is related to my Rheumatoid Arthritis which was triggered by my father's abuse. Many of us have health issues; we just have to navigate the world with the cards we were dealt and **find peace in being** grateful for the blessings in our life. I am always grateful for indoor plumbing; remembering my grandmother's outhouse and her washtub for bathing. I am always grateful for food, remembering all the times as a child when we didn't have food to eat and went to sleep very hungry. I am always grateful for a safe home and a bed. My father's alcoholism put us in the position of homelessness several times. I am grateful for heat in the winter. I remember not having heat in a home in Tennessee and warming with the kitchen stove.

In my case, I have had to handle most of my health issues without the assistance of modern drugs. I just happen to have severe allergies and to be very drug sensitive. I could only handle Tylenol when I had a total knee replacement in 2009. Nevertheless, I am alive today because of outstanding medical care and amazing healthcare providers. I am blessed.

"Life is like a game of cards. The hand you are dealt is determinism; the way you play it is free will."
Jawaharlal Nehru

1984 - Christmas Eve - my 2nd Angel Encounter

I was sitting up in bed reading. An angel, with wings and a flowing gown surrounded by light appeared levitating in my bedroom doorway. The angel didn't speak but talked to me in thoughts. She told me that she had come to answer my prayers and that I was pregnant. She told me that I would have a son and that I should name him **Jonathan which means God's promise**. This angel also told me some things about my marriage and my pregnancy. She told me that it was my choice to keep my baby or not, and that Larry and I would never again be intimate. Jonathan was born nine months later. He has been and is today, a true blessing and a great joy. Jonathan and I shared so many happy times while he was growing up. Every day I was grateful to have my own child; even though Jonathan is high functioning on the autism spectrum. We did everything together until Larry separated us in our vengeful divorce custody battle.

"Having a baby is a life-changer. It gives you a whole other perspective on why you wake up every day."
Taylor Hanson

In 2018, Jonathan invited me and my dog, Mindy, whom Jonathan adores, to live with him. This has been a blessing. In the three and a half years I have lived with Jonathan, I have had 9 of 12 major eye surgeries and several other surgeries. I have a very rare genetic eye condition - Pseudoexfoliation Syndrome. Jonathan was noticeably an older soul from birth. He doesn't need people, nor does he have any friends; however, he has been very kind to us. Jonathan loves Mindy and he kindly walks her outside three times a day. This gets him outside regularly. Mindy is a blessing for Jonathan. I rescued Mindy; she rescued Jonathan. They share a beautiful human-animal connection of pure love.

Jonathan did graduate from University of Illinois School of Engineering with honors and he has a great job as an electrical engineer. Since COVID he has been working from home, which has really isolated him and he has become less tolerant of interruptions and requests.

We are blessed. I certainly never expected my child to have to take care of me; however, I am grateful that he did offer. Being visually impaired is very scary. Every day I say, **"Thank you God that I can see and that I am mobile for another day."** And every night when I give Jonathan his good night side hug, I thank him for two or three things that he has done for Mindy and me during that day. No matter how bad things are, **there are always things to be grateful for.**

"There is always something to be GRATEFUL for."
Rhonda Byrne

7 - Teaching
Blessed by Children

Having spent 35 years in classrooms, I have learned that schools should be places students identify their strengths by exploring their talents from a young age instead of all children following the same path and studying to pass tests. We have been given different gifts. Banning books is what folks do to further their control. Testing only makes administrators look good or bad. Schools should be for children and for their best learning practices. I was so blessed to have taught in a great school district with fantastic fellow teachers where most parents deeply cared about their child's success. I was blessed to have taught children and to have learned from children.

Having spent 35 years in classrooms, I am blessed with many memories, some most wonderful and some that still pull at my heart-strings daily. Some of my former students have looked me up on Facebook, remembering that my name was P Diane Chambers. Angie T. is one of those blessings - we regularly correspond. I had her in third grade. She has two grown sons now. Then there are the memories of the children I lost to death. Mike D. who died at age eight from leukemia. Chris L. who drown by getting stuck in a whirlpool drain. Annie H. who died as a young mother from cancer; and, Michael R. who took his own life. Michael was one of my third-grade students. He was a small boy with a happy disposition and who loved to spend his time with the girls. Michael's dad regularly complained to me and demanded that I insist that Michael only spend his time with boys. Michael's father, a high-powered tall business man, was very forceful.

After high school graduation, Michael came back to visit me. I was teaching in a different school now, but in the same District. Michael had grown into a handsome averaged sized young man and I was delighted to see him and visit with him as I worked in my Science Lab. At the end of our visit, I hugged Michael and wished him well in college. The next morning, Michael's mom called me. Michael had hung himself that night. She and I both realized that my visit with Michael was him coming to say good-bye. Mrs. R. was so sweet telling me how much her son loved me. Nevertheless, all I could think about then and to this day is what could I have said or done to change Michael's mind - to stop him. What clue had I missed ? Every day of my life, since this drama, I keep asking myself, what could I have said ? And, then, there was the sorrow for Mrs. R., burying her only child. I still ask myself most days - why is Michael gone and why I am still living as an old lady ? What is my purpose ?

The best lesson that I think all of my students learned from me is that **"the impossible only takes a little longer"**. It was my daily goal, especially when I taught science, to have students believe that nothing is impossible. I was always telling them about things like a flying plane - folks initially said that human flying machines were impossible. For me, the most important element for real education is unlocking curiosity and a desire to stretch the boundaries in knowledge and learning. Amazing things happen when a child has unlimited learning. To this day, I can still hear my students parroting me - saying - **"The impossible only takes a little longer."**

"When we believe in the impossible, we can do all kinds of extraordinary things." Madeleine L'Engle

"Knowing how to think empowers you far beyond those who know only what to think." Neil deGrasse Tyson

"The good thing about SCIENCE is that it is true whether or not you believe in it." Neil deGrasse Tyson

8 - Environmentalist
Over-Population and Climate Change

Realizing that HEART and EARTH are spelled with the same letters, I have always known that it was my duty to be a voice and a VOTE for our planet and the creatures and plants who dwell here.

I am a steward for our Planet, our children, our creatures, and our trees who inhabit this planet. This is where my money goes every month - to 41 charities. I WALK MY TALK daily, and I have since 1980. Besides my 41 charities, I also belong to eleven environmental and wildlife organizations. I give monthly to our local Food Bank and support Durham Meals On Wheels with my painting sales contributions. I give to several holiday food programs, two of which are for our Native Americans. We can all do something. Time is a great gift to give to charities and moral causes.

You are either part of the solution or part of the problem.

Are you a steward of God's creation ? The earth is not healthy.

"If the people in the pews who profess a love for God's creation are not protecting earth, how can we expect anyone else to ?" Rev. Cannon Sally Bingham

I am astonished daily by the number of Americans who see themselves as good Christians; and yet, do nothing to help protect our planet for the next seven generations. People seem to be so self-centered, only concerned about getting the resources they want. And, if a weather drama isn't in their backyard, they ignore all the severe weather and weather suffering around the world. Since 1980, I have been a small voice speaking out about CLIMATE CHANGE and saving our planet. Today, 2022, in my small 55+ community yard, I have small chemical-free pollinator gardens. My plants aren't impressive to humans; however, they are an island of safety for pollinators. This summer, butterflies have been scarce in my yard. Seeing species become extinct means that soon humans will also face extinction. Humans are already dying from drought and famine. How sad for our children that we didn't care enough to share, use carefully, exploit less, and care more about their planet. **We have allowed greed, waste, and wealth to be more important than survival.**

"God commands us to be good Earth stewards." "Listen to the cry of the earth." Archbishop Justin Welby

One of the simple lessons that I taught elementary students in Science is that the **WATER AND AIR ON EARTH TODAY ARE THE SAME WATER AND AIR USED BY THE DINOSAURS.** People see rain and snow falling from the sky and assume that it is new water. It is in reality water just being recycled in the Water Cycle.

SCIENCE IS SURVIVAL IMPORTANT !!!

"Look into Nature and then you will understand everything better." Einstein

"They shall not hurt or destroy in all my holy mountain; for the Earth shall be full of the knowledge of the Lord as the waters cover the sea." Colossians 1:15-16

The BIBLE has over 100 verses about taking care of the Earth. **"Behold, to the LORD your GOD belong heaven and the heaven of heavens, the earth with all in it."** Deuteronomy 10:14

The chemicals that are dumped on lawns and in toilets don't just disappear. They stay in the water cycle and kill many live organisms. Someday we are going to kill ourselves with all of these poisons.

OVER-POPULATION drives CLIMATE CHANGE - **since 1980 I have been aware of the over-population of our planet and of CLIMATE CHANGE.** I have been speaking about them to deaf ears.

We are killing our planet and driving CLIMATE CHANGE with too many people. I have been speaking about this for over 40 years. We have wasted so much precious time. While we desperately need to limit population, Republicans ban abortion ! Why can't humans see that limiting our population is what is needed for survival of our planet. We need immediate action ! It is **time to start regulating the male body** - the male seed; world-wide. A woman can only have a child every nine months. While a man can impregnate hundreds of women in a year. As a species, trying to survive, we can no longer tolerate the irresponsible actions of men seeding more than two children.

"One man can impregnate 9 women every day for 9 months. Those are 2430 pregnancies. One woman can only get pregnant once within 9 months, even if she beds 9 men every day within 9 months. That's only one pregnancy. So clearly, society is placing the birth control responsibilities on the wrong gender. Science is busy making pills, and hormone altering devices for the

wrong person. Meanwhile, the culprit is known and on the loose."   Allies Academy

"A woman has 1 baby in 9 months; A man can create 2,430 pregnancies in the same time."   Stella Dimoko

OVER-POPULATION is Spaceship Earth's most dire crisis. The Republican party and the Catholic Church are the two largest organizations, world-wide, blocking birth control and our survival action. **Earth has twice as many people living on it, than it can sustain.** This is a scientific fact which seemingly intelligent humans are ignoring as they continue to populate like rabbits. There will be no inhabital planet left for the next seven generations. This will be the result of self-centeredness and greed.
https://eluxemagazine.com/culture/articles/human-overpopulation/

Water and food shortages are already showing up all over the world. We are headed towards a world-wide water crisis.   https://www.ifpri.org/publication/world-water-and-food-2025

"August 15, 2022 – Record high food price have triggered a global crisis that will drive millions more into extreme poverty, magnifying hunger and malnutrition."
https://www.worldbank.org/en/topic/agriculture/brief/food-security-update

These are the truths that so many choose to ignore. You can't be a REAL CHRISTIAN or a moral soul while ignoring these facts about our planet and the needs of the people trying to live on our planet. **If you are a moral soul, you will be helping to limit population and to help struggling humans to survive.**

As an environmentalist, even though I have had **SOLAR** energy for 12 years already, I still try to save energy.

During the winter, our thermostat is set at 67, and during the summer our thermostat is set at 78. I also use passive solar energy by opening, closing, raising and lowering our blinds to control the sun's energy coming in our windows. It isn't that we can't afford higher energy bills. I conserve energy because I think about the next seven gerenations that will inherit the earth. We turn off lights in rooms that we aren't using. We buy LED lights for inside and outside usage. We understand the impact that fossil fuels have on our planet, so we try to live as a model for others.

"Even with all our technology and the inventions that make modern life so much easier than it once was, it takes just one big natural disaster to wipe all that away and remind us that, here on Earth, we're still at the mercy of nature."
Neil DeGrasse Tyson

9 - Hell
There is a HELL for sinners.

When I was awake and stable, I was amazed by my thoughts about my six lovely walks to Heaven and that God decided I was to stay on Earth. I was wrapped in a warmth of comfort and love. As I relayed my experiences about Heaven and walking with Jesus, I assumed everyone's experiences would be the same. Nurse after nurse assured me that many NDE (near death experiences) are undesirable, scary experiences. Folks return from the other side terrified. They tell their nurses that they have been to Hell. I was so surprised. I am not anyone special. I am just a very imperfect, sinful human trying to do my best daily.

Yes, there is a Hell for the liars, cheats, and abusers. Sometimes the Karma happens on Earth. Other times, Karma happens after death. In these cases, the soul is tormented for the bad choices that were made. There is justice for those who do not care about others, for those who are greedy, and for those who ignore the needs of others while having the means to help. Like the balance of nature, there is a **balancing of the soul**. Souls that have lived good lives and have taken care of others and who have taken care of our planet are rewarded with great blissful peace. Those who have not cared for others and who have been selfish, are terrorized by being chased though darkness by their own **shadows of greed** and **self-centeredness**. The evils that were done by a soul now become the evils that haunt the soul. **Our choices do have consequences.**

"The soul always knows what to do to heal itself. The challenge is to silence the mind." Caroline Myss

The Bible has 50 Bible verses about sinners going to Hell.

"God has pronounced that the penalty of sin is spiritual death and separation from GOD in a place of judgement called Hell; for the wages of sin is death."
Bible Romans 6:23

DEATH is simply the doorway between the physical and the spiritual world; as is birth.

Souls will live many lives. Old, wise souls have already lived many lives. Most of us are in stages between young and old souls.

Your behavior and actions or inactions during your earthly, human experience determines your experience when you pass through the doorway of death. You have FREE WILL as an earthly being and you alone decide how you will live your life and how you will spend your time after death. Some believe that you will choose the life (human experience) you are born back into the next lifetime.

Some people also believe in a difference between the soul and the spirit. For these folks, the soul lives within the body and interacts with everything in the physical body using our five senses. They see the spirit as the part that has a relationship with God. In my near-death experience and human experiences, I view the soul and spirit as one. I understand the soul/spirit as going through the doorway of death into heaven or hell; according to the choices we have made. In my near-death experience, my soul/spirit arose from my body, walked a light of bliss to meet Jesus. I entered Heaven for short periods of time before returning to my body and my human experience again.

I don't know which souls go to heaven or which go to hell. I know that the concept of **HELL** is mentioned in many religions: Roman & Greek mythology, Egyptians,

Islam, Buddhism, and Hinduism. In the Bible, there are **seven deadly sins** that can send your soul to hell.

1. **Pride** - vanity, inflated sense of one's accomplishments.
   Can be overcome by being HUMBLE. Pray and serve.
2. **Greed** - excessive desire for material things.
   Can be overcome by being GENEROUS. Donate.
3. **Lust** - illicit sexual desire or craving.
   Can be overcome by being PURE, guarding your heart.
4. **Envy** - jealousy towards another.
   Can be overcome by being THANKFUL.
5. **Gluttony** - indulging in excessive eating and drinking.
   Can be overcome by being MODERATION.
6. **Wrath** - anger.
   Can be overcome by being PATIENT. Restrain your emotions.
7. **Sloth** - laziness, lack of effort.
   Can be overcome by being DILIGENT - having a schedule.

Besides these guides for living, the Bibles also has the **Ten Commandments**.

1. You shall have no other Gods before Me.
2. You shall not make idols.
3. You shall not take the name of the LORD your GOD in vain.
4. Remember the Sabbath, and keep it holy.
5. Honor your father and mother.
6. You shall not murder.
7. You shall not commit adultery.
8. You shall not steal.
9. You shall not bear false witness against your neighbor.
10. You shall not covet your neighbor's house or any of his belongings.

I don't know if the concept of HELL developed because of people having near-death experiences like me or if it developed as a way for people to cope with the horrors people see and experiences they have on earth. I am one of those people shocked and perplexed by the double standards of folks who proudly and loudly call themselves Christians and in the same breath support people who openly break the Ten Commandments and who openly boast about committing all Seven Deadly Sins. How can people ignore the scandals and the mockery ?

It is my understanding from reading, that the Ten Commandments are valid for all people. One surely can't be an authentic Christian or an authentic Jew while supporting sins. In spite of these rock-solid guides, some people seem to get away with everything and avoid consequences on Earth. I guess HELL awaits them. Some people are involved in multiple scandals and escape all penalties. I am one of the people who is regularly stunned by these events and the lack of consequences. This is when I have to remind myself --

For we know him who said, **"Vengeance is mine; I will repay."** And again, **"The Lord will judge his people."**   Hebrews 10:30 ESV

I guess - being an imperfect human - I want to see the vengeance (consequences) and to know that it happened. I want to see the person punished for extortion, thievery, collusion, ethics violations, tax fraud, abuse, child trafficking, and other crimes against people. I **do believe that there is justice in the end. And, maybe that justice is called HELL.**

Do you VOTE to help God's people and to take care of God's planet; or do you vote to profit yourself and your way of life ???

10 - Wars

Divorce & Middle East

I spent over $275,000.00 in legal fees from 1999-2005 for my divorce and custody battle. I had to refinance my townhouse every year for five years. Even so, I always gave to the hungry, homeless, and to our soldiers in the Middle East. I did without many things and kept using my old things so that I could help others. I was never a fashion plate, so this wasn't a sacrifice. I helped the hungry and the homeless locally. And, I sent thousands of pounds of toiletries and snacks and holiday treats to our soldiers in the Middle East - all as a way of honoring my brother, Johnny, who had been drafted to Viet Nam. I am anti-war; however, I am very respectful of our soldiers who serve. Jonathan, my son, regularly helped me with these large packages; usually 70 pounds, the military limit. We made and filled Halloween bags, Christmas stockings, Valentine pouches and Easter sacks to spice up our packages. In every box we sent extra hard candy, children's books, and treats for the local children. I sent sewing items and cloth for the women. I normally worked with Special Forces Platoons and Army Chaplains through an organization called **AdoptAPlatoon.** I have many awards. Notes about how I helped children and women in the Middle East were my greatest rewards.

My divorce was painful and lonely. I spent six years in Family Court. Larry, Jonathan's father, was determined to see me penniless for divorcing him. I walked out of the marriage with less than I went into the marriage with; and yet, I had worked all 20 years of our marriage. I wanted so badly to be free of my loveless, sexless marriage. These six years are when I learned firsthand about the **political injustices** in our Court System. DuPage County in the western suburbs of Chicago was

Republican controlled and it was as crooked as any part of Chicago. DuPage County was set up so that no father would have to give up the family home or to pay child support; and, no mother would get custody of her child/children. Larry, being a gun-carrying NRA Republican, had the power of the unjust Court system behind him. I found myself entangled in a relentless custody battle which I eventually lost, even though the court appointed psychologist wrote that I was the better parent to raise Jonathan.

Several of my long-time friends dumped me for fear that they might be called to Court as witnesses. My pain and suffering through this ordeal were worse than any of my father's abuse or my medical issues. When I lost my only child in court, I wanted to take my own life. I was so numb from the financial rape and from the devastation of Jonathan being taken away. I was crushed. Isolation was my only company. Tears flowed night and day. The light in my spirit had dimmed out and I had no will to look for the blessings in this situation. I just wanted to walk in front of a train and end it all. Jonathan had been the only good part of my marriage and he was the light of my life. I had devoted my life to children and now my own child had been taken away - by evil corruption. I had no family for support. Friends dropped away. I was alone and I couldn't understand why God had saved my life to let me walk through this lonely Hell on Earth. There was nothing left to live for. My health worsened. I had spent more time and money in Court than a vicious criminal. My losses were great. And, the most heart-breaking, Larry isolated Jonathan and I was powerless to prevent this. Larry never bought Jonathan any clothes or supplies. Larry used the child support money for himself, and he sold the family home pocketing 20 years of profit. When Jonathan would come to visit me every weekend, I would see his needs and buy Jonathan what he required, while still paying child support. I kept getting raped financially and emotionally. Every day, I would tell myself to **hang on for one more day**. More sorrow, Larry didn't want Jonathan to go to college, since he didn't have a college education himself, and since he knew how I valued education.

Just hang on one more day. I would tell myself. In the ashes of my life, God put his arms around me. My hopelessness slowly bloomed into tiny bits of courage and I decided that there was nothing but sorrow to keep me in Illinois, so I would move, but where to ?

H.O.P.E. = Hold on, PAIN ends !

"Sometimes the bad things that happen in our lives put us directly on the path to the best things that will ever happen to us." Nicole Reed

11 - Caring For Others
2004 Teacher Humanitarian

"The high destiny of the individual is to serve rather than to rule." Albert Einstein

Making life a little better for those less fortunate than I had been my goal all of my life, even as a child. I have known hunger, abuse, and homelessness first hand, so helping others is deeply personal for me. It has always been my desire to help others. I even helped when I felt so helpless and useless myself.

Having survived a "death experience", I believed that I had been given bonus time as a reward for spending my first 52 years taking care of others and that I had more work to do. I believed that God had a special plan for my life and I needed to pay attention to be led by God forward to find my **"Big Job"**. In the midst of my life draining divorce and custody battle, I became the **2004 Teacher Humanitarian for the State of Illinois** chasing the goal of helping others. My School District nominated me. I am a humble, behind-the-scenes worker. Being in the spotlight is very uncomfortable for me. I never do anything for the praise, but it is nice to be appreciated occasionally.

Even during times of my own great fear and my own great hardship, I felt it was still important to reach out and help others. However, as the years passed, and I continued to volunteer and give generously to others, I grew to realize that my extra time was a gift to me to use my talents and time to become the **JOY-FILLED woman that God always intended me to be**. I have been a wife for 32 years, a mother for 37 years, a public school teacher for 35 years, a summer Park District counselor for 10 years, the oldest of four children for 75 years, and a loyal friend to some for more than 50 years. I have met my obligations to society and voted in every election for over 50 years. I have usually given almost 20% of my income to charity and I have tax records as proof. I have wanted little and lived simply. During the final chapter of my life, I am trying to become the authentic person I was always meant to be while continuing to be **a passionate voice for children, animals, trees, and our planet that children will inherit**. I can't explain why some die so young and why I was given so many bonus years. I have been blessed with doctors and medical folks who wouldn't give up and let me die. I often thought it would have been much better to die than to walk through the hell of my divorce and custody battle. However, there is still much work to do and there are still many who need help.

"IF YOU CAN'T FEED A 100 PEOPLE, THEN FEED JUST ONE." Mother Teresa

When you do things to help others, you can be in a zone that takes you away from some of your pain, physical and/or emotional. It is a blessed place of peace. Helping fills your heart and soul with comfort. It can be your happy place.

"Part of being a person is about helping others." Regis Murayi

Since moving to Durham, I have continued my support of people with less. I have 41 Charities that I have continued to support monthly with auto draft donations. When I sell my Watercolor Paintings, 100% of the sale price goes to **Durham Meals On Wheels**. I don't take the cost of materials from the donation. I give the entire sales price. In 2021, I donated $1,485.00 to Durham Meals On Wheels; and in 2022, I donated $1,780.00 to them. I donate yearly to **Save A Child – Embrace Uganda,** to **The Seeing Eye,** to holiday meal baskets for our Native Americans and to numerous other amazing charities. There are so many worthwhile ways to help others and to help save our planet. If one can't afford to give money, volunteering time is an extraordinary blessing. Volunteers are the lifeblood of every charity.

NPR - 10/19/22 **"One million seniors in the U.S. live below the poverty level."**

Any profit from this book will go to **DigDeep.org**. There are 2.2 million Americans who still do not have running water in their homes. Much of the work of Dig Deep is in the Navajo and Appalachian areas of America. **Running water changes lives forever.**

"We never know the worth of WATER till the well is dry." French proverb

"Water is life, and clean water means health." Audrey Hepburn

I have a heart that feels the important need to **feed the hungry**, **take care of children**, **provide medical care for others**, and **care for our planet**. I donate monthly to our local **Food Bank**, food items and money. I give to the Durham Meals On Wheels program regularly. My Charities are the first item on my monthly expenses. I am not a fashion plate and I live simply; cook daily, rarely eat out, and don't travel, so my funds can go to help others. I have had the same furniture and drapes since 1976. I am not bragging. This is my choice. This is my walk. My life is about more than me. **This is what God would have me do.**

12 - Move to Asheville

Healing my broken heart and my broken back.

I launched my "daring adventure" (Helen Keller), after much research, to move to Asheville, North Carolina where I didn't know anyone. My mission would be to look every day for the blessings in the ashes of my shattered life and to give thanks. I had suffered years of physical and sexual abuse; and I had survived. I had died and survived. I had walked through family court hell for six years and survived. Now, God would help me start a new life in a new place. God would restore my body, my soul, and rekindle my spirit.

Fleeing from the corrupt DuPage County Court System and an ex-husband who would not leave me alone, I moved to Asheville, North Carolina, unaccompanied and alone. I did know that this university city was liberal and cosmopolitan. This gave me great hope. I believed that even a shy person like myself could find a new start and happiness in the (OLLI) Osher Lifelong Learning Institute at UNC Asheville. Learning brings me such joy. How blessed humans are to have a brain that will allow them to continue learning even as we age past 65. (While in Asheville, I took 144 classes at OLLI)

In the past, my schedule was developed to accommodate others and their needs. I had lived a demanding life of trying to please others; especially in-laws, who hated me because I wasn't Catholic and they believed that I condemned them to hell by not being Catholic. It became routine and comfortable, like my old garden shoes with a hole in the right toe, to work tirelessly to try to please others. Now, I could leave this exhausting role behind and devote some time to exploring my talents and the new possibilities open to me. I no longer had to spend thankless days doing what was expected of me. God had opened my eyes, my heart, and lifted my spirit. I knew things wouldn't be easy, being a single senior woman in a new place in the south without a safety net of a friend or family. However, I had never had the luxury of a safety net or a family to help me in the past. As I had done before, I would rely on God for guidance. Besides, I was counting on UNCA and their senior program to give me the roots I didn't have in family.

Initially, I fell prey to several pretending to befriend me; yet, just wanting money. Sometimes my fears shadowed my hopes. Nevertheless, I was determined to make the blessings of this new opportunity work. I would believe that I could succeed and rebuild. I would replenish my courage from God. And, I would count my blessings hourly.

Once again, I would try to turn tragedy into triumph. And, I would do this by focusing on **being grateful** and **counting my blessings**.

In 2005, I started painting again. For the 20 years while I was raising Jonathan and in Family Court, I never painted. I devoted my time and talents to Jonathan. Once I started painting again, my Chicago friends were shocked to see my paintings and couldn't believe that I had put this gift away for 20 years. Nowadays, and for as long as I can see, I consider myself a Watercolor Artist.

The total sale price for every painting I sell goes to **Meals On Wheels**. I don't even take out the cost of my materials. Seniors shouldn't have to worry about eating; nor, should children.

Those of us who are blessed can share and bless those with less.

"Be willing to share your Blessings. The only riches that last are the ones that are given away." David Khalil

I built a ranch home in Asheville on a half-acre of sloped land. Almost all land in Asheville is sloped. Daily, I spent countless hours working the land, mainly turning it into a wildlife habitat for small wildlife and for pollinators. I did plant nineteen blueberry bushes and I did have three fountains which sometimes attracted black bears. However, usually my wildlife was smaller, like possums and birds. I did have a bobcat that made one of his dens in my small wooded front yard. He made regular appearances on my driveway, but never threatened me or my small dog.

In Asheville, I wrote myself a plan for staying grateful and happy:
1. **BE GRATEFUL EVERY DAY** - for every blessing: my sight, my mobility, money to pay my bills, places to go, a vehicle 12 years old and still working, classes to take, good medical care, and pictures to paint.
2. **BE PASSIONATE ABOUT PEOPLE AND PROJECTS** - Jonathan, my dog, learning, painting, gardening, volunteering, and helping others.
3. **STAY ACTIVE** - swim, garden, attend functions - even by myself, learn, and paint. Focus on what I can do, not what I can't do.
4. **DO THINGS DIFFERENTLY** - even if I only drive a different way home or use a new vegetable in crockpot soup, this would keep my brain active.

In June of 2008, while I was pulling weeds on one of my slopes, I fell backwards down the slope and broke my back in three places, two upper breaks and my L5. Initially, I was bed ridden and the spine surgeon wanted to operate. I felt sure that once I could sit up and walk with a brace on that I could heal my back in the pool. For a month, I laid in bed picturing being in a pool and healing my back. So, a month after my fall, I started faithfully going to the YMCA pool. Luckily, it was only eight minutes from my home. And, being an old pool, the deep end was seven feet deep. For 365 days, I went to the pool daily and dog paddled for an hour, no noodle, just dog paddling in the deep end to stretch out my spine. I allowed my spine to hang without pressure or gravity. After the first week, my spine surgeon took an x-ray and he was surprised, my spine was already beginning to heal. Then an x-ray was taken in two weeks, and there was even more improvement. I was faithful to my pool therapy daily; my belief that I could heal my spine without surgery; and to my gratitude that I could still move and that I was healing. After one month of pool therapy, my spine surgeon was stunned, the healing was remarkable. Another x-ray after two months showed my spine was continuing to heal and my surgeon said that I wouldn't need surgery if I continued my daily dog paddling in the pool for an hour. Medically, I am very compliant. My pool time was my first priority every day for a year. Again, I made medical history. It is now, 2022, I am three inches shorter because of my fall; however, I have never had any issue with my spine and never any backaches. **The pool was therapeutic, and so were my spoken words of gratitude** and **my affirmations. I focused on healing and did the daily hard work to heal. I was very blessed.**

13 - EVIL Always Seeks Good
Ignorance Allows Evil to Thrive.

On earth, unfortunately, evil finds goodness and tries to destroy it.

> **"Evil can have power in this world because of gullible, simple-minded, ignorant, foolish people."**
> Dietrich Bonhoeffer, German theologian against Hitler

I was starting to have a problem with my neighbor, Josh; I found daily trash in my yard and plants were dug up and stolen at night. In Asheville, North Carolina, when a next-door neighbors' home was foreclosed, the angry young man decided to take out his frustrations on me; a single, senior handicapped neighbor, living alone, who had helped their family regularly. Not only did Josh destroy the inside of the house they lived in; but Josh also dumped destroyed discards over the fence nightly into my yard. Each morning I would find pieces of wallboard, cabinet doors or shelves, garbage scrapes from their meals and their daily living, beer cans and bottles, and even strips of carpeting and flooring that they were ripping up from their floors. One night Josh tossed a closet door that he had hammer holes in and a broken toilet tank top over the fence. Another night, he tossed shutters from the outside of his home that he had ripped off and broken before tossing them into my yard. I called the police, but they were no help. Besides throwing house destruction junk over the fence into my yard, Josh would sneak into my yard and dig up my prized plants and steal them. Each morning, besides the garbage tossed over the fence, I would find new holes in my yard where plants had been dug up during the night. The man's ego couldn't handle that he had failed to meet his financial obligations so he turned his anger towards me and made my life miserable for several months. **Ignorance !!!** Male ego run amuck !!! Josh did make my life miserable. The yard between us was a 15 foot slope with a 50 degree angle. Since my yard was steeply slopped, I had to hire someone three times to help clean up the debris on my slope. Hate, like the hate unleashed by this young man, is seen in our news daily. Young souls can be very destructive, unkind poor neighbors, and unproductive unhappy citizens.

"And good neighbors make a huge difference in the quality of life. I agree." Robert Fulghum

This is the same kind of behavior I see all across the United States. Mindless people making choices that don't help themselves. Most of the poor folks in the United States vote Republican; yet, the Republicans rarely support issues or bills that improve their impoverished life. Republicans want folks to stay poor so that there are plenty of bodies to fill military positions. Wars keep Republicans rich. War is the Republican's biggest money maker.

I wonder why some people dislike "liberals." Liberal Democrats brought you: **Social Security, Medicare,** Medicaid, Healthcare Reform, Food Safety, The Peace Corp, Vista, Job Corp, Civil Rights, Women's Right to Vote, Equal Rights, The Voting Rights Act, Equal Pay Act, Federal Deposit Insurance Company, Banking and Wall Street Regulations, Security and Exchange Commission, Federal Reserve System, Anti-trust Legislation, Funding for Science, Medical and Engineering Research, Space Exploration, National Science Foundation, National Institute of Health, Head Start, School Lunch & Breakfast Programs, 8 HR. Work Day/40 HR. Work Week, Overtime, Unemployment, Protection for the Environment,

Increased Numbers and Support of National Parks and Wilderness Areas, Endangered Species Act, FEMA, Veterans' Benefits, GI Bill, UN, NATO, Marshall Plan, Vehicles Safety Requirements, The Department of Agriculture, Amber Alert, Amtrak, Public Beaches, Public Busing Services, Business Subsidies, The Census Bureau, The CIA, Federal Student Loans, The court System, DAMS, Public Defenders, Disability Insurance, The Department of Energy, The EPA, Farm Subsidies, The FBI, The FCC, The FDA, Fire Departments, FEMA, Food Stamps, GARBAGE Collection, Health Care, Public Housing, The IRS, Public Landfills, Public Libraries, The Military, Sated & National Monuments, Public Museums, NASA, The National Weather Service, Public Parks, Police Departments, Prisons & Jails, Public Schools, Secret Service, Sewer Systems, Snow Removal Services, Public Street Lighting, The Department of Transportation (Highways, Roads, Bridges), USPS, Vaccines, Veteran Healthcare, Welfare, White House, The WIC Program, State Zoos, Reduced Emissions, and Fuel Economy Standards (CAFE), TVA, Federal Loan Program, PBS, NPR, the Internet, and Economic Growth (Democratic Presidents: Roosevelt through Obama). **Clinton even balanced the budget. In 2019 we will add $1 trillion to our national debt = Republican spending.** I am so proud to be a Liberal. Unfortunately, no matter how much the Liberals provide for the poor and other Americans, the **ignorant remain ill-informed**.

If the poor Americans would wake up, most could have the AMERICAN DREAM of building a society where nobody starves or goes homeless, and where everyone is treated fairly, receiving a living wage and affordable or free healthcare. Unfortunately, ignorance follows hate.

When a country cares more about entertainment and athletes than education, the result is a country of ignorant people who are easily led by evil and hate. And, these uninformed folks attack the good people trying to help them. Ignorance seeking power becomes unruly and dangerous.

What Does the Bible Say About Forgiving Someone Who Has Harmed You? Matthew 6:14-15 NIV, **"For if you forgive other people when they sin against you, your heavenly Father will also forgive you. But if you do not forgive others their sins, your Father will not forgive your sins."**

The Apostle Paul says in Romans chapter 12, **"Bless those who persecute you; bless and do not curse. Do not repay anyone evil for evil. Do not take revenge, my dear friends, but leave room for God's wrath, for it is written: "It is mine to avenge; I will repay," says the Lord.**

"If we wish to rebuild our cities, we must first rebuild our neighborhoods." Harvey Milk

"He who has a good neighbor has a good morning."
Danish Proverb

14 - Move to Durham

In 2017, following five years of multiple surgeries and being homebound for eleven and a half months of those five years, Jonathan, my son, talked me into moving to Durham, North Carolina, to be closer to him. There were so many things that I loved about Asheville; however, my evil neighbor had made me afraid to live alone in a regular neighborhood. I had lived alone for twenty years until my neighbor lost his home to foreclosure and started abusing me by trashing my yard and stealing my plants. This neighbor had moved; however, the helpless fear that he instilled in me stayed.

"Loneliness is about the scariest thing out there."
Joss Whedon

When Josh and his wife moved in next door to me, they were a young couple with two jobs, two kids, two cars, and their first home. When their home was foreclosed on, this couple had one job, three kids, and two cars. Plus, they ate out regularly and the wife shopped daily. They were clearly immature about many things. And, his meanness made my life miserable.

"Lonely is not being alone, it's the feeling that no one cares." Swatantra Saxena

"Do not be afraid; our fate cannot be taken from us; it is a gift." Dante Alighieri

From 2012 until 2017, I had undergone a total knee replacement (done twice), a broken shoulder, two major rotator cuff surgeries, three eye surgeries, knee scoping and stem cell procedures and three PRP knee treatments. These kept me home-bound for most of a year in five years. Under these conditions, living alone became very lonely, especially with a neighbor terrorizing me because of his own over spending and losing his home. My knee replacement was extremely difficult as I couldn't keep any pain meds down. I did my total knee replacement recovery just using Tylenol. Two years after my knee replacement, because my body hadn't liked the prothesis and had encapsulated the knee in scar tissue which made the knee difficult to bend, I had the replacement redone. Unfortunately, even though this second knee replacement surgery was done completely differently, my results were the same. My right knee only has 60 degrees of bend or flexion even after two years of PT (physical therapy). People need 110 to 120 degrees of bend to go up and down stairs, to get in and out of a car, or to ride a bicycle. The normal healthy knee has 135 degrees of knee flexion. My right knee is very limiting.

"The most terrible poverty is loneliness and the feeling of being unloved." Mother Teresa

"It's easy to stand in the crowd, but it takes courage to stand alone." Mahatma Gandhi

In May of 2017, I put my home on the market via local social media and I sold my home in twenty-four hours because of the amazing yard and all the lovely flowers that I had planted on my half acre. I really hated to leave my wildlife refuge and all the critters that called my yard home. And, I hated to leave the UNCA community, my Painting community, and my amazing Church. Grace Covenant Presbyterian Church is one of those rare churches that walks their talk and puts mission before building ego. They really follow Jesus' walk. However, I no longer felt safe, even with nice, new neighbors. I needed to make a future in a safe place.

I moved to Durham and moved into an apartment with all of my quickly packed belongings. I looked for a home to buy. I bought a resale in a 55+ community. I was there for six months and another two surgeries when Jonathan suggested that we live together. Jonathan was madly in love with Mindy, my dog, and she was crazy about him. I was lucky to be connected to both. We looked around and decided to build a home together in another 55+ community. In February of 2018, we signed a contract and then set about getting Jonathan's home ready for market. Through this entire process, Jonathan was so amazing - working full time ten hour shifts five days a week, working on his home, helping to squeeze my crowded possessions so we could find room for his things. We literally had couches stacked on top of couches. Luckily, my two-car garage held a lot of belongings with room for me to still park because of Jonathan's amazing engineering skills. Jonathan was remarkable in the way he adjusted to all of these changes; they weren't easy for him being on the autism spectrum. Mindy was crazy in love and so thrilled to have Jonathan with her every day. From March, when we sold Jonathan's home in one weekend, until October of 2018, we lived like sardines. None of us minded; we had a plan. **We were grateful that we were going to be living together.** Jonathan and Mindy filled my every day with a new-found joy and gratefulness. I was blessed.

"Give thanks for all of the opportunities that even our struggles bring." Steindl-Rast

"Through the eyes of gratitude, everything is a miracle."
Mary Davis

15 - Forms of Evil
Jealousy, Lies, Gossip, and Dishonesty

Walks to Heaven don't protect a human from earthly encounters with evil young souls. One is not even protected if they are handicapped and visually impaired.

Building our new home in Durham, North Carolina, turned out to be a nightmare for my son and me. Right in the middle of the process, our builder sold the community to another builder. Our project manager was overseeing (very poorly) the building of forty homes at one time. (I could write a book just on the horrific experiences in this process). My son and I faced many challenges in the procedure: mold, water main breakage, carpeting laid before bathroom tile was put in, water turned off after the final inspection before closing because of leaks, shades that came down when opened or closed, a leaky outside wall that had to be torn down on the north side of our home in January, and so on.

At the same time our home was being built so was our next-door neighbor's house. The second Sunday we met them, two parents and a twenty six year old son, I handed them one of my Art Cards because it had all of our contact information on it. From that moment, the relationship changed. Initially, we noticed them bragging more and being more boastful. Plus, they also started lying. This would be a pattern that would continue and worsen. Little did we know how jealous they were of us. It would turn out that they were jealous of my art and of Jonathan's good job.

"Comparison is the thief of joy." Theodore Roosevelt.

*Neighbors - Gossips and spreads falsehoods out of jealousy. Stalks and urinates on our front bush.

Our home was built while our next-door neighbor's house was being built. Home buyers were allowed to visit their home construction site on Sundays when workers weren't present. Each Sunday that we saw our to-be-new neighbors during the building process, it was the same - **bragging, boasting and lying.** Once we moved in, our jealous neighbor even told other neighbors that her son worked where my son worked. As it turned out, her son didn't work at all. In fact, in two years, I only saw him outside of their home twice. Stories that this woman told got back to me as neighbors checked in with me. Our jealous neighbors claimed that I was stalking them because I was taking photos in my yard. In truth, many of my photos I took were used to send to friends in other states of my new home, our new yard and my Holiday decorations. Plus, I take pictures as watercolor painting studies. This family also claimed that I had stolen their property. In fact, the man came over several evenings after 9:30 p.m. and stood on our porch waiting for me to come home from the pool. The jealous neighbor's husband would follow my car into our garage - knowing that Jonathan was at work. The first time, I got out of the car, thinking something was wrong. He screamed loudly at me about stealing his property. **My neighbor fear was back.**

I have moved 37 times in my lifetime and only twice have I had any fear of my neighbors. The second night that he followed me into our garage screaming, I stayed in my car and closed the garage door. He ran out as the door was closing. The third night that I came home from the pool about 9:30 p.m., he stood on our sidewalk, unzipped his pants, and urinated on one of our bushes. Today, one can still see that one of our front bushes is missing half - the half he killed with his acid urine. I called the police and the next day these neighbors, both individually, filed civil suits again me - claiming that I was stalking them and that I had stolen their property. I had never been in their yard. They also claimed that I was antisemitic even though I had had Bernie Sanders' campaign signs in my yard and my car was covered in BERNIE Sanders' magnets. They insisted that I was lying to the neighbors about them. I never shared with neighbors what they were saying and doing to me. We went to court and it was apparent to all in the room, that they had done this before. Several court folks even said this to me as I was leaving court. My jealous neighbors tried to get the judge to disallow me from participating in any community events that they might attend. The judge threw the cases out of court.

And, it turns out the property that I was supposed to have stolen was a property stake which we later found in the bushes. The landscaping folks, who mow our grass, must have tossed the stake into the bushes. Jonathan took the stake over to our neighbors. With all the problems in the world, how could two people start a court battle over a lot line stake when we all have a landscaping company maintaining our lawns ? Later, I would discover that my jealous neighbor had an Art degree, but had never done anything with her degree. Art was a hobby for me and I had enough paintings to have an Art Website. People in our community would come to know me as the Watercolor Lady who sells her paintings very reasonably and donates 100% of the sale price to **Durham Meals on Wheels.**

"Envy is the declaration of inferiority."
Napoleon Bonaparte

No matter how evil my neighbors have treated me, nevertheless, I have put heart shaped crystals in our windows facing their home. Every morning and every evening when I open and close our blinds, I say a prayer for them. This is as God would have it.

"The jealous are troublesome to others, but a torment to themselves." William Penn

*Jealous neighbors and retaining wall. On the south side of our home, our neighbors elected to have the retaining wall between our small yards put on our property. This has been very problematic for us causing a water drainage problem in our yard. We even had to have a $1,700.00 dry river bed put in so that we didn't have a mosquito swamp in one part of our yard. When it was our turn to have a retaining wall put on our north side, I had the choice of having the retaining wall put on our property or on our jealous neighbor's property. Even though I had been treated badly and am still treated badly with false gossip, I elected to have the wall put on our property so as not to cause a water drainage problem in our jealous neighbors' yard. I sacrificed a foot, the entire length of our yard to help my neighbor; even though, this neighbor had taken me to court over a property line stake. And as a gardener, it wasn't easy to give up my land. However, as a real Christian, the right thing is always the right thing to do. I am sure my dishonest neighbors never bother to share how I have prevented them from having a water drainage problem in their yard. Their yard is the lowest property on our side of the street for blocks. **They are blessed to have me as a neighbor.**

"He that has revenge in his power, and does not use it, is the greater man." Wellins Calcott

"Doing the right thing even when no one is looking is easy if I remember that I am not in this life alone and that my task is to please God … not people." Sandra C. Bibb

"Let us do the right thing, there are those who will understand." Anthony Ejefoh

*Community neighbors try to get into paid community events without paying. Some evil is thought to be clever and harmless. Yet, it is basically stealing, cheating and a great lack of respect for others, especially when one lives in a $400,000 - $700,000 home and can afford all of their needs and wants and can easily pay an $8 - $18 entry fee for an event. Sadly, I am aware of this cheating regularly in my 55+ Community. I just don't understand it.

This is Free Will at work. We each have the opportunity daily to be honest or to cheat. And, we will each experience the consequences of our choices in the spiritual world.

"Free Will carried many a soul to hell, but never a soul to heaven." Charles Spurgeon

"There's too much tendency to attribute to God the evils that man does of his own Free Will."
Agatha Christie

16 - Twelve Eye Surgeries

It is very scary to have a very rare eye condition, especially when one is so visual. Nevertheless, **I seem to see more clearly than most.**

My one in a million eye condition is **PSEUDOEXFOLIATION Syndrome (PXF)**. This is a genetic condition, (LOXL1 gene). "Pseudoexfoliation syndrome (PXF or PEX) is an age-related systemic syndrome that targets mainly ocular tissues through the gradual deposition of fibrillary white flaky material from the lens, mainly on the lens capsule, ciliary body, zonules, corneal endothelium, iris and pupillary margin." "Pseudoexfoliation glaucoma (PEG**) is a common cause of blindness worldwide** and tends to be more progressive and serious compared to primary OAG (POAG) = open angle glaucoma."
https://eyewiki.aao.org/Pseudoexfoliation_Syndrome#:~:text=Pseudoexfoliation%20syndrome

This is the rare eye condition that I have. My DNA says that I am Scottish, Irish, and German. This PXF condition is only on a Scandinavian gene. I guess there was a Viking in the wood pile. We each have to deal with the cards we were dealt.

In my case, the flaking away of tissue causes a lack of tissue to hold lens. I have had lens implants four times and other serious implant related surgeries: a detached retina and a shunt implanted in my left eye to reduce the high pressures of 50, normal is below 20. High eye pressures kill off the optic nerve. Each surgery has been very scary for me. I look at everything with eyes that may never see again. None of my painting friends seem to be aware of how close blindness is for me. None of them seem to relate. Each day I look at things and try to remember how they look; in case I will never see them again. I used to look at things and wonder, how do I paint that. Each day, I try to remember exactly where things are in my home in case this will be the last time that I can see them. It is a heavy weight to carry around daily - blindness worries on my shoulders.

Duke Eye - part of Duke University - did a video about me and my PXF condition and so many experimental surgeries. Erin, the videographer, had great compassion for me, especially as she heard Dr. Rosdahl speak about what a difficult case I am because I am so allergic to so many drugs and to most of the eye drops. Numbing drops, instead of anesthesia have been used for some of my surgeries because I get so sick from anesthesia. The numbing drops burn like acid when they are applied to a raw open eye. Besides the surgical pain and the recovery pain, I have also had to deal with the **great fear of going blind** as I have to sign a waiver before each surgery stating that I may be left blind. I not only have to sign a waiver, but I am also told by each eye surgeon personally that my surgery is experimental with my condition and that I may be blind after surgery. I don't even know how to describe the intense fear - each day thinking about what things look like and where they are in case this is the last day that I have sight. The worry knot in my stomach is always there.

As a visual person who considers herself a Watercolor Artist during this last chapter of her life, becoming blind is very frightening - **horrifying**. We all walk the scary paths of the unknown. Most of the folks around us can't understand the fears we face. Some of our paths we walk alone. Some are blessed to have folks in their life who understand their fear and their pain. In spite of my worry and fear, as long as I can, I will paint.

My Art Web Site -
https://pdchambers.wixsite.com/artist/home

Any painting that I sell, 100% of the sale price goes to Meals On Wheels.

After one of my lens implant surgeries, I wasn't able to wear glasses or to drive for eleven months. One's freedom is really hampered when you lose your driving independence. Some days it was very difficult to hang onto hope and to promote my own healing. Mental health and hope are so important in healing.

"You have to live through the bad days to get to the good ones. Hang in there …. " Kenji Miyazawa

"If you are going through Hell, keep going."
Winston Churchill

"Everything you've ever wanted is on the other side of fear." George Addair

In my case, on August 5th, 2022, I have just survived my 12th eye surgery. This one was without anesthesia because of my drug allergies. The shunt in my left eye hurts like a spear is poking me in the eye. September 5th, I am a month out of surgery and my eye is still red, swollen, bleeding a bit and painful. I feel like I have a pencil stuck in my eye now. It does improve some every day, little by little. My eye is still making a lot of mucus daily. Surgeries without the help of the usual drugs are very challenging. Plus, my eye surgeries are difficult because I have had so many eye surgeries. My goal is not to whine about my eye surgery or to even talk about it wherever I go. We each have burdens to carry. In my case, when I am asked about my eye surgery, I try to answer truthfully, but hopefully.

On September 8th I will be having the first two layers of sutures removed. My eye is healing. And, to myself -- all day long, I say, *My eye is healing. Thank you God that I can see clearly.* I have even been playing two games with my sight. Every crepe myrtle tree, that I see, I say ... *Thank you for the beautiful crepe myrtle. Thank you that I can see clearly.* Crepe myrtle trees are abundant in North Carolina and are blooming around August. Even without the blooms, crepe myrtles are easy to identify by their multiple shiny trunks.

And, then other times during the day, I sing to my left eye. ...
If you are happy and you know it, heal your eye.
If you are happy and you know it, heal your eye.
If you are happy and you know it, then your eyes will surely show it.
If you are happy and you know it, heal your eye.
These are behaviors that help keep me in a positive place and prevent me from falling into the hole of self-pity. They are just ways for me to remind myself **to be positive** and **to be thankful**. These are small optimistic distractions of joy. They may help you come up with ways to turn your disappointment, sorrow, and worry into pleasure and hope.

For now, I put six kinds of eye drops in my eyes, 24 times a day. And, I do consider myself very blessed to still be seeing. And, I will daily be grateful to my skilled surgeons who are helping me to continue to see. **My eye is healing.**

September 11th, I didn't get my eye sutures removed as I developed an eye infection on September 6th. This was a great disappointment. Now, hopefully, I will be able to have the first two layers of sutures removed on September 19th. For now, I try to stay hopeful and I faithfully put in all of my eye drops on time. I have made so many eye drop charts. Each time I see one of my eye surgeons, my eye drops are adjusted and I have to make a new eye drop chart to accommodate the changes, usually weekly. **I am blessed that I can still see** and that I have outstanding medical care. Many, world-wide, are not as fortunate as I. **I am grateful** for my sight and my medical eye care.

"Choose to see the world through grateful eyes. It will never look the same way again." Doe Zantamata

"Gratitude brings more to be grateful about, so today I make the point of expressing gratitude for everything in my life." Louise Hay

17 - Eyes and Body Donated to Science

I had first donated my body to science in 2007 as part of my Living Trust. However, with my new more severe and rare medical conditions, in 2020 my body donations became more specific. My rare eyes are going to Duke Bio-Sight and my body is going to Duke Medical School. One doesn't need their body after death. **YOUR SPIRIT/SOUL IS ETERNAL.** Your body is simply a vessel for a single life-time, for one human experience. You don't need a coffin or a grave. At death, your soul will leave your body vessel and enter into the spiritual world. You will have a spiritual experience, negative or positive based on how you treated people and how you cared for this planet while you were here. At some point, your spirit can decide to have another human experience and will then get a new body for this new human experience. In your new human experience, you may be a different gender, a different race, and even live on a different continent. Think about this as you decide how to treat other people. **Most everyone deserves respect.**

If you are uncomfortable donating your body to science, at least give your organs to save a life. And, consider this alternative: **TheLivingUrn.com**

Why waste your resources on an expensive funeral ? Think of the hungry you could feed, the homeless you could shelter, and the sick you could care for with the price of an expensive funeral. As I know, when you go to meet Jesus, you will be leaving your body behind. Only your soul will go through the door of death to the spiritual side.

You could also be cremated. Cremation uses flames and heat to reduce the human remains to bone fragments and cremated remains. Cremation is also more affordable than a funeral with a casket, a grave, and a head stone. None of us are so important that we need a permanent memorial for mourning.

"There shall be eternal summer in the grateful heart."
Celia Thaxter

In nature, a body of a human or an animal begins to decompose several minutes after death. Once the cells are deprived of oxygen, their acidity causes chemical reactions to begin. This is Nature's way of recycling the elements into other usable forms. The energy isn't lost, just recycled into substances that can be reused by nature.

In my case, I have my eyes donated to Duke Bio-Sight and the rest of me is donated to Duke Medical School as anatomical gifts. This is my way of giving back even after I am gone. This is my way of paying forward for all of the excellent medical care that I have been privileged to have. Plus, it makes my passing easy for Jonathan. All of the paperwork is done. He has a folder with copies of the signed paperwork, numbers and two phone numbers to call. I hope my gifts will help others with their eye and medical challenges. After my body is used as a cadaver, I will be cremated and my ashes will go on the Duke Gardens' recycling pile. I will probably become food for plants. Being a gardener, I can't think of a better way for my energy to be used.

"People living deeply have no fear of death." Anis Nin

While this is happening, my soul will hopefully be in Heaven. Heaven is such a blissful place to be. I recommend being an **honest, caring person** so that your soul goes to Heaven. Being thankful and being grateful helps each of us to appreciate our blessings so that we don't fall into the GREED trap. Care about your fellow human and offer a helping hand when you can. Be thankful that you are in a position of helping another. Let your voice and your actions stand for morality and honesty. Be grateful.

Be Thankful, Grateful, and Helpful.

"You are comprised of 84 minerals,
23 elements, and 8 gallons of water
Spread across 38 trillion cells.
You have been built up from nothing by
The spare parts of the earth you
Have consumed, according
To a set of instructions
Hidden in a double helix and small
Enough to be carried by a sperm.
You are recycled butterflies, plants,
Rocks, streams, firewood, wolf fur, and
Shark teeth, broken down to their
Smallest parts and rebuilt into our
Planet's most complex living things.
You are not Living on Earth.
You are Earth.   Aubrey Marcus

"We are all connected. To each other, biologically. To the earth, chemically. To the rest of the universe, atomically."
Neil deGrasse Tyson

"The root of JOY is gratefulness."   David Steindl-Rast

18 - Autonomic Neuropathy
2020 - 2-5 years

2022 - Mayo Clinic has given me about two to three more years; there is no treatment and no cure. So, I have to share my story now, or not at all. In 2020, my new cardiologist connected the dots and diagnosed my condition to be Autonomic Neuropathy. Of course, God will decide when I am leaving this earth.

My cardiologist said, *"You have the best heart that I have ever seen in a 74 year old - this is the good news. The bad news is that you have a Ferrari driven by a drunk - this is the bad news. There is really nothing that I can do for you. You have Autonomic Neuropathy which means you have 2-5 years to live."* Yep, this is how blunt he was. He did tell me to take off a lot of weight. Another battle for me since menopause.

Autonomic neuropathy **occurs when the nerves that control involuntary bodily functions are damaged**. It can affect blood pressure, temperature control, digestion, bladder function and even sexual function. Neurologic function declines gradually over time. The autonomic symptoms often become debilitating. Autoimmune diseases like rheumatoid arthritis can become causes of Autonomic Neuropathy." "Autonomic neuropathy type II (HSAN2) **is a rare genetic disorder."**
https://www.mayoclinic.org/diseases-conditions/autonomic-neuropathy/symptoms-causes/syc-20369829#:~:text=Autonomic%20neuropathy%20occurs%20when%20there,function%20and%20even%

It doesn't matter what condition you have that takes you from this earthly planet. God will decide when you leave. You, however, can decide what gifts you leave behind. Why waste your resources on a casket, a plot, and a head stone ? If you are lucky enough to be a senior, decide how you will give back for the long time that you have lived and the many blessings you have enjoyed.

Since I have always had major medical issues to deal with, I have always been aware of how important good medical care is. Even though my medical care is limited by my sensitivity to drugs, I am still walking this earth at age 75 because of the outstanding medical care I have had. I have been blessed. I wish everyone on earth could be blessed with good medical care. Instead of looking at all of the major medical conditions I have, I try to focus on the great medical care I receive that allows me to continue to live. I try to pay it forward in many ways. My anatomical gifts will be one way.

For now, I run to the restroom, 24 times a day. I have been tested and had two years of PT on my bladder and pelvic area. My bladder is fine and my pelvic floor is surprisingly strong for my age. It is the autonomic neuropathy at work destroying the nerves. My nerve signals to my brain are malfunctioning. I realize that my body functions could be worse. I am grateful that I can manage this now. I am grateful for indoor plumbing and toilet paper. And, I am blessed to live in a home with more than one bathroom. I am blessed to live with Jonathan in a really nice home. I could never afford this home by myself. I am blessed and thankful.

This is my situation. Others suffer with other afflictions - addictions, cancer, lost limbs, heart conditions, blindness, strokes, respiratory disease, diabetes, Alzheimer's, mental illness, obesity, HIV/AIDS, & others. Even with all of these health crises, health organizations in the United States and around the world are beginning to note **CLIMATE CHANGE** as the top threat to human health.

https://mphdegree.usc.edu/blog/3-global-public-health-threats/

Now, you understand why God will be looking at how you have treated others and how you have treated our planet. How are you caring for planet Earth ? Are you dumping poisonous chemicals on your lawn - that will seep into the water supply ? Are you wasteful ? Do you sincerely recycle ? A friend of mine was telling me about his friend who works in a recycling center. Often this worker sees that the recycling can is used for a 2nd garbage can and not for recyclables - this can ruin a lot of recyclables, a whole truck load, even more. People seem to be unaware of the ripples of their bad behavior. **Do you promote renewable energy ?** I have done without many things so that I could have SOLAR energy for 12 years, in Asheville and now in Durham.

Lack of vaccinations is also becoming a top health threat in the US.
https://www.wwmedgroup.com/blog/top-5-health-threats-to-americans/   Feb. 26,2022

So, you can see that **what you do** and **what you don't do** as a human has an impact on other humans and their survival, not just your survival. **We are all connected.** In your next life, you will walk in very different shoes. Again, consider, how are you treating others . Be caring of those with less. Share. Be grateful for all that you have.

"An attitude of gratitude brings great things." Yogi Bhajan

Sometimes, it is difficult to see the light at the end of the tunnel and to be grateful. A little trick I used to get myself out of a funky place is to text or email a friend to just check up on them. I try to send a picture I have taken from my yard or of my holiday decorations to add a bit of cheer with my **simple message**. (You should see my Halloween decorations. I decorate for every occasion as if I still had a classroom so I always have time appropriate pictures to include with a short message.) "How was Friday's doctor appointment ???" "Just checking in, how do you feel today ???" "Headed to the grocery store, can I pick up anything for you ???" **My photos** and **messages are simple, but magical.** They get my focus off of me and my health worries. And, hopefully, they add a bit of cheer to someone's day. We all appreciate being remembered. I am grateful that I can add a little smile to someone's day.

"In the depth of winter, I finally learned that within me there lay an invincible summer." Albert Camus

19 - SPEAK TRUTH
Be a Light for Humanity

People don't realize how hard it is to speak the truth to a world of people who would rather believe lies. I am surrounded by passive, apathetic folks. This makes it so easy for power to conquer and control them. Hitler learned this. Only truth can save us from the rich owning and controlling everything, even our **water and food supplies**.

Imagine how advanced society would be, if parents encouraged their children to go to a science class every Sunday instead of forcing them to go to church.

Anonymous

I say this as a retired Science teacher and an ordained Presbyterian elder. The truth is in science not MAN-MADE religion that is often the framework for man to control others.

"Three things cannot be long hidden: the sun, the moon, and the truth." Buddha

"I am the Way, the Truth, and the Life" Jesus

Human Rights initiative under the auspices of Robert F. Kennedy Human Rights. "To speak truth to power means **to demand a moral response to a problem, rather than an expedient, easy or selfish response**. The phrase speak truth to power carries a connotation of bravery, of risking either the status quo, one's reputation or livelihood, or the wrath of the person one is confronting."

"The Importance of Truth. Truth matters, both to us as individuals and to society as a whole. **As individuals, being truthful means that we can grow and mature, learning from our mistakes**. For society, truthfulness makes social bonds, and lying and hypocrisy break them. **People who lie repeatedly often have a desire to be in control**. When the truth of a situation doesn't agree with such control, they produce a lie that does conform to the narrative they desire. Such people may also worry they won't be respected if the truth can leave them looking poorly."
"Truthfulness is the greatest and most important of all human virtues. Truthfulness means **to speak the truth habitually**. A truthful man will never tell a lie. ... In life, learning to be honest and eliminating the need for lies can help to clean up your conscience and your relationships." American Friends = Quakers

"To thine own self be true, and it must follow, as night the day, that thou canst not then be false to any man." Shakespeare

"The truth is rarely pure and never simple." Oscar Wilde

Your words and your values can only be aligned if you speak and live the truth. And, this has to start with being honest with yourself. Then, you must weed out

88

the false information you hear. If you are honest and truthful, your life will show it. Others will know that they can trust you. Do you define yourself with **HONESTY** and **TRUTH** ?

"Do the right thing, even when no one is looking. It's called integrity." Bow Nuttaa Mahattana

HONESTY (TRUTH) has always been the first of my four core values that I have lived by my entire life. Honesty and Truth are rock-solid characteristics upon which to build a good person, a good soul. **God appreciates TRUTH**.

20 - False Christians

"I like your Christ, I do not like your Christians. Your Christians are so unlike your Christ." Mahatma Gandhi

"You might as well try to hear without ears or breathe without lungs, as to try to live a Christian life without the spirit of GOD in your heart." Dwight L. Moody

I have not written this book sooner in my life because it is a heavy burden on my shoulders to speak the truth as it was given to me by Jesus and to try to be polite. Unfortunately, at the rate that the United States is decaying, politeness is no longer possible. I was tasked with this job so I must say the truth.

You will know that you are a fake Christian if you support and/or voted for Trump, the anti-Christ. If you doubt my words, ask yourself, how many times have you been to Heaven ? You are a Fake Christian if you support the Republican party. **Their platform is built around keeping the impoverished poor and uneducated and controlled, while making the wealthy richer**. They do not feed the hungry, shelter the homeless, or care for the sick. In fact, they keep drug prices so high that people die because they can't afford the drugs they need and the food they need to live. As a Republican, your actions and lack of actions speak louder than your prayers. Jesus would not recognize you as a Christian. **The Republican party and the Evangelicals are cults that do not care about people. They gather to worship power, money and greed.** Christ would be the first to condemn them.

If your political party and your religion are exclusive and do not embrace everyone, you are not Christian. Yes, it is that simple.

I am very imperfect; however, I always know what is right and what is wrong. **Right is always right; wrong is always wrong. I know that GOD is inclusive.**

*BIBLE - the Bible is based on stories told orally for 30 – 90 years after events happened and before these events were written down as the people didn't know how to write. The Bible has been written, rewritten, edited, re-edited, and translated from dead languages by men. Example: Folks believe that the human population came from Adam & Eve; yet, Adam and Eve had only three sons; Cain, Abel & Seth. Today's science tells us that all Humans originated in Africa and had dark skin. The Bible is a collection of 66 books from 40 authors. There is evidence that it has been altered over time. God will not ask you if you know any Bible verses. **God will know if you have taken care of others and his Planet.** The Bible is a history and a guide. If you can only cite Bible verses and don't live as a Liberal, you have missed the point of Jesus' teachings. Jesus fed the hungry and cared for the sick. He didn't collect wealth and/or power. Mega churches would not please God. **Jesus was inclusive.** He wanted God's people taken care of and God's planet cherished.

*Adam & Eve - some explain the story in this way -- "Adam and Eve were not the first human beings; in fact, were not actual people. Adam represented one group or tribe while Eve represented a different group or tribe. These tribes intermarried and thus was born a merging of religions and beliefs, the birth of what is now Christianity." This is an interesting idea from a friend of mine. And, it shows how the Bible can be interpreted in different ways. I believe in SCIENCE which GOD created. I believe that the first humans evolved in Africa and had dark skin, as the world-wide National Geographic DNA Study from 2005-2015 proved. We evolved from these humans and **we are all immigrants with black roots. And, the Bible**

91

was written about people with olive/brown skin. Jesus had olive/brown skin. Jesus was not WHITE. The Bible is not written about white people.

*Lessons to Learn - if you don't learn your lessons now, you will have to learn them in your future lives. Your soul will be chased in death by your bad choices. You have God's gift of Free Will to decide what your afterlife will be like.

*Are you a Fake Christian --- read this list and decide ...... You are a FAKE Christian

> ***If you park in a HANDICAP PARKING SPACE without being handicapped or having a handicapped person in your vehicle.**
> *If you are dishonest.
> *If you worship yourself and always have to be the center of attention.
> *If your word is meaningless.
> *If you hurt others, especially children.
> *If you are a racist and discriminate.
> *If you are homophobic.
> *If you ban books.
> *If you stand in the way of education so you can keep people ignorant so you can control them.
> *If you ignore homelessness, hunger, and sickness in others.
> *If you support criminals and crimes.
> *If you ignore rape and women's rights.
> *If you allow power to take advantage of people.
> *If you fly an American flag, but do not respect the Constitution and the Bill of Right and our Capitol.
> *If you make money supporting wars.
> ***If you ignore or deny Climate Change.**
> *If you don't believe people working 40 hours a week deserve shelter, food, and healthcare.
> *If you work to prevent the truth from being taught

in schools.

*If you support children being brides.

*If you brag and boast constantly and loudly, drawing attention to yourself.

*If you are stingy and selfish.

*If you fight and vote against liberal ways that help fellow humans and protect children.

*If you attend a fancy church while ignoring the hunger, sickness, and homelessness all around you.

*If you ignore that children live in homes with unsafe water and insufficient food.

*If you talk the Bible, but do not follow Jesus' teachings.

*If you lie.

*If you cheat others.

*If you fail to protect children.

*If you expect privileges for your family, but not for others.

*If you talk more than you listen. (you have two ears and one mouth)

*If you aren't trustworthy.

*If you get your news from FOX NEWS, an entertainment channel.

*If you support someone who is unethical.

*If you back someone for office who is immoral.

* If you lack a conscience.

*If you are disrespectful.

*If you lack integrity.

*If you profit from war.

*If you are an Animal Trophy Hunter.

*If mock those less fortunate than you.

*If you do not tithe: Leviticus 27:30, Matthew 6:21, & many more Bible verses.

*If you support the Republican Party.

*If you have double-standards.

***If you voted for Trump.**

*Republican are fulfilling the prophecy by worshipping the anti-Christ as Revelations said they would. Trump is clearly the Anti-Christ. He is the worst kind of young soul - lying, racism, sexism, sexual assault, treason, dividing

America, corruption, cheating, regular scandals and double-standards to gain wealth and to stay in the spotlight. Trump hurt people and workers - **ignored the pandemic**; **stopped funding of Social Security; pushed for lower wages for migrant farmworkers**; suspended all union elections; **obstructed workers' rights to fair union elections**; narrowed the joint-employer standard; encouraged off-shoring; tried to help employers avoid paying over-time; **prevented millions of workers from receiving overtime**; undermined the job security for service workers; weakened standards for mine safety inspections; **allowed employers to steal worker's tips**; passed Tax Cuts and Jobs Act which benefited the wealthy; **repealed a requirement that employers report workplace injuries and illnesses**; and made it easier for contractors who violated basic labor and employment laws to be awarded contacts paid for by taxpayer dollars. See all 50 ways that Trump worked to enslave workers and make the rich richer. https://www.epi.org/publication/50-reasons/

Not only did Trump hurt workers and seniors, he also hurt our environment. Trump **made it easier to lease public land for oil & gas drilling, enabled the expansion of offshore drilling**; proposed making 85% of the National Petroleum Reserve in Alaska available for oil & gas drilling; **exited international Climate Change cooperation**; reversed a rule that prevented taking sand from protected areas to replenish other beaches; ; **narrowed pollution safeguards for lakes, rivers, tributaries & wetlands**; proposed speeding up the environmental review process seeking Oil & gas drilling permits in national forests; **weakened toxic pollution & water rules for coal plants**; rolled back rules designed to prevent accidents at chemical facilities; delayed issuing & enforcing new ozone pollution standards; **weakened climate standards for new vehicles**; withdrew a proposed rule to protect groundwater near uranium mining sites; approved the building of the Dakota Access pipeline; **weakened monetary penalties for automakers who fail to meet fuel efficiency standards;**

proposed opening the protected Tongass national forest in Alaska to logging & road construction; **authorized oil & gas leasing on the Arctic National Wildlife Refuge's coastal plain**; proposed changes to rules governing the high emissions from power plant startups, shutdowns, & malfunctions; rescinded policies requiring companies to offset environmental harms to public lands; **reversed climate rules for the electricity sector**; which seeks to tally the money spent & lives lost as a result of climate change; **repealed a rule to prevent coal mining companies from dumping waste in streams**; ordered federal agencies to review rules impeding energy production, resulting in numerous environmental rollbacks; **rescinded requirements limiting super-polluting refrigerants**; weakened protections on hunting, capturing and killing migratory birds; **rolled back fracking regulations that protect drinking water on federal & tribal lands**; weakened regulations on pesticide use in National Wildlife Refuges; halted a rule that tightened air pollution standards for offshore drilling operations; **weakened environmental reviews for major projects & exempted projects from review**; discontinued a National Parks Service policy discouraging the sale of plastic water bottles in parks; **proposed weakening pesticide regulations meant to protect agricultural workers**; proposed to weakened grazing restrictions on public lands; **declined to ban a toxic pesticide**; eliminated a rule to prevent waste by requiring oil & gas operations on federal lands to limit venting & flaring of methane.   See all 75 ways that Trump worked to help the wealthy at the cost of our environment. https://www.theguardian.com/us-news/ng-interactive/2020/oct/20/trump-us-dirtier-planet-warmer-75-ways Clearly, Trump has no concern for people or for God's planet. He is not a Christian. The people that support him are young souls who do not care about people or earth. **Trump is a destructive young soul motivated by greed.** Trump's supporters are young souls seeking wealth, control and power.

> "God gave us Free Will, and we may choose to exercise it in ways that end up hurting other people."
> Francis Collins

*Bible Study groups wouldn't give to local Food Bank. In my own 55+ community, we have two large Bible Study groups, a women's group and a men's group. During the Pandemic, I approached both groups about collecting $5.00 from each member at their monthly meeting to donate to our local Food Bank. The men's group at least discussed this idea. The head of the women's group was adamant about not collecting $5.00 from each member. She claimed that asking her members to donate $5.00 monthly for our local food bank would cause some members to not attend her meeting. This was said by a woman who runs a Bible Study group in a community of $400,000 - $700,000 homes. I am sure that Jesus would not be pleased. The men's group declined also. Obviously, these are people who do not walk their talk. **They are fake Christians.** To the credit of the woman who runs my Painting group, we donate $5.00 a person on a weekly basis for our local Food Bank. Over several years, we have contributed thousands of dollars and it has not been a hardship for any of us. We are blessing the less fortunate while enjoying the blessings of our talents.

> "If you do not live what you believe, you will end up believing what you live." Fulton J. Sheen

Fake Christians have the most lessons to learn. These are people who are young souls that are self-centered, selfish, and unaware of what God wants them to do.

21 - Double Standards

Being a woman, and now a single, handicapped senior woman, my life has always been filled with Double-Standards. Here are some examples of double standards.

In 1979, when I went through my first divorce and tried to get a mortgage on my own - I had been teaching full time for nine years. I was finally given a mortgage to buy our home from my first husband because as the banker said, **"You are attractive enough, I am sure that you will be remarried within a year or two ."** The fact that I had a Master's Degree and had worked full time for nine years wasn't a consideration.

In 2006, when I built a home in Asheville, one of my neighbors had a landscaping business. Although my lot was half acre, I had only a small part that needed weed-whacking. Because of my RA, weed-whacking on the slopes at age 60 was difficult for me. I hired my neighbor - he charged me $40.00 an hour. My yard took less than an hour. His reasoning was that **he was a professional and should be paid professional wages.** However, when I, as a retired PROFESSIONAL TEACHER, baby-sat for them or Dog Sat for them (I had a part-time job of dog sitting in Asheville), I charged them nothing. And, they never offered to pay me. I was just being a "good neighbor". A single senior woman was expected to give her services away; while a man expected to be paid. After two years, when I brought this contradiction up to this family, it was sadly the end of our friendship.

*Pro-Life - Sister Joan Chittister "I think in many cases, your morality is deeply lacking if all you want is a child born, but not a child fed, not a child educated, not a child housed. That's not Pro-Life. **That's Pro-Birth.**"

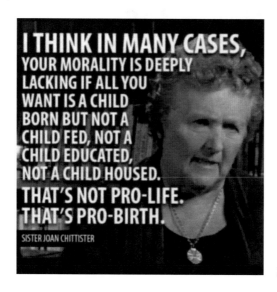

Sister Joan Chittister

*Anti-abortion & Pro-guns ....   HallArt.zans.co

If you believe your girlfriend deserves a safe abortion, but not other women; you have double-standards. If you withhold birth control from women, you have double-standards.   Our planet is already over-crowded. It is much crueler to allow children to be born and then to have them starve to death because of drought and hunger.

*No birth control for women, but Viagra for men.

* Pro-Birth, but not Pro-Life

Nick Anderson

*Bird Watchers - claims to adore birds; yet, fill their own yards with chemicals that kill birds and their food supply. Their true value is neighbor impressive landscaping over wildlife. They do not walk their talk or stand with Mother Nature.

*Audubon Yard visit and Backyard Birders Power Point. I belong to a community Bird Lover's Group. The leader of this group encouraged me to invite our local Audubon Society to survey and appraise my small yard as a bird-friendly habitat. I had already had my yard registered as a National Wildlife Habitat. I paid my $50.00 and had the survey. The Audubon Society didn't certify my yard. They wanted some of my plants replaced with native plants. After this yard survey, the head of our Birding group, who had encouraged me to have the survey done in the first place, asked me to prepare a Power Point Presentation about my Audubon experience. I hadn't put a Power Point together in 17 years and I had started having regular eye surgeries. Consequently, I had to spend hours and hours preparing my presentation. I even had beautiful pictures of my yard to explain the pros and cons of the Audubon Society's survey. Two years later, my beautiful presentation has never been shown. As soon as our head Birder saw my presentation and saw the number one item that the Audubon Society objected to in yards (except mine) was chemicals, my presentation was shelved. Our head Birder would rather look at birds in the wild than make his own well-manicured yard a safe place for birds. It is difficult for me living in a world where people don't walk their talk. People only care if they are not inconvenienced and if they don't have to change their own behavior. You can head a Birder's Group without having a Bird-friendly Habitat yard because of your usage of many harmful chemicals. And, so it is with most of the members of this Backyard Birders. They prefer to have weed free grass than safe habitats for birds.

*Folks in my 55+ community live in a $400,000 - $700,000 home; yet, try to get into community events free - lie about having paid to attend the event. I live in a 55+ Community with my son (who is only 37) because of my many health issues. We both paid for our smaller home. As everyone knows, the prices of homes everywhere have skyrocketed. In our Community, we have some amazing women who work endlessly to put on community events at very reasonable prices. Even though the prices are low and many make donations to help keep the prices low, a few folks always try to get into the events free. (If there was a financial need, our community would take care of it.) These are people who have no respect and who are clueless about all the work that goes into an event. These are **CHEATERS**! The line they most often use is that they did register for the event and that they did pay on-line. Both are not true. What kind of a person - with sufficient financial means - cheats their neighbors and their community ? In my case, I always buy two tickets - even knowing that my son will probably be working - but hoping he can run in for dinner. My goal is to be supportive of these ladies and their amazing creative work. If ever I hear of someone who wants a ticket and couldn't get one, I give them Jonathan's ticket. One has to wonder, did the cheating folks gain their financial means by cheating others ? Also, during the warmer months, Jonathan and I swim in our community outdoor pool from 6:00-7:00 p.m., during his dinner hour from work. (He works second shift.) When our community has an outdoor musical event, I buy two tickets even though Jonathan and I will not be attending, but will be swimming for a short part of the concert time. I try to be fair. The pool is next to the grassy area used for outdoor concerts. I just don't understand the mind of a cheater.

I admire and love some of the folks in my conservative 55+ community; I just don't understand their values and their double standards. They clearly do not follow the examples Jesus set. **God sent Jesus to Earth so that humans would have an example to follow of how to care for each other**. Clearly, most don't understand this. Folks simply look for folks who mirror their own selfish ways and values. How difficult is honesty and living moral values ? God will judge people, not me. I am just a voice for the children, for the disadvantaged people, for the animals, for the wildlife, for the trees, for our water, for our air, and for our soil. They have too few speaking up for them and voting in their favor.

God knows that I am one of the vital voices - a voice that Jesus directed me to be.

*ADOPTION - Evangelicals, Republicans, & Catholics want all of these children born, they are against birth control and/or abortion. However, how many unwanted children have they adopted ? It is all loud propaganda and no responsibility. It is ignoring the over-population of our planet. I, personally, don't know of any Evangelical, any Republican, or any Catholic, in North Carolina, Illinois, or Indiana who has adopted a child or children. I am sure there are folks in this country who have adopted; I just don't know any.

*In Vitro Fertilization - Catholics & Republicans: I have a lovely friend with three beautiful daughters. Two daughters are married with children. These families are staunch Catholics & Republicans. The youngest daughter, unmarried, was hearing her biological clock tick away and decided she wanted a child like her sisters. With no future husband insight, she decided to go for In Vitro Fertilization, even though the Catholic church pronounces it "Immoral". https://www.usccb.org/issues-and-action/human-life-and-dignity/reproductive-technology/begotten-not-made-a-catholic-view-of-reproductive-technology After several rounds, the daughter did get pregnant and delivered a healthy, beautiful baby boy. All four families are thrilled with the new addition to their family. However, they are not thrilled enough to give other women the right of control over their own bodies. **They all still vote Republican.** Humans are incredibly selfish and very self-centered. Unless, something helps them, most won't support it. Plus, people like to take moral stands without any intention of helping with the consequence of their choice. In 2022, the United States has about 407,493 children in Foster Care.

Unfortunately, a **"disproportionate representation of Black and American Indian children"** is in the US Foster Care System which is also a money maker. Republicans, Evangelicals and Catholics insist that all children be born; however, after birth they vanish when the child's care comes into question. Is this what Jesus would do ?

*Immigration - unless you are a native American, **you are an immigrant** ! If you want to close our borders and deport the immigrants, are you going to **plant our crops, pick our crops, clean our public buildings,** or **work in a restaurant** ? The people who yell the loudest about immigrants and closing our borders, are the same folks who hire, at low wages, immigrants to work in their businesses and in their homes. This issue, like abortion, is used as a smoke screen so that folks don't realize that the rich are getting richer and the poor are getting poorer. It is a bait and switch issue. Too bad so many Americans are ignorant about this truth. How easily Americans are led to hate immigrants. Yet, immigrants do so much of the work that keeps us fed. **Jesus was an immigrant.**

Matt. 2:13-23 points to the importance of immigrants and the ethical necessity of open borders. How quickly the Bible quoters forget these passages.

The most amazing phenomime is the **first generation immigrants** that I know who are embracing the Republican party and embracing closing our borders. Since they are here, they don't want others to have the same opportunity. ? What a blessing that Liberals believe that all people deserve the same chances, same opportunities, and same privileges. **I am proud to be a Liberal, like Jesus.**

"What separates privilege from entitlement is gratitude."
Brene Brown

*Republican & Evangelical double-standard ......

Anonymous

Do Republicans and Evangelicals just ignore these double standards ? I guess when one belongs to a cult, you don't examine its values even though God has given you an amazing brain for critical thinking.

I am grateful that I use my brain daily to weed out the untruths and lies. I am grateful that I use what I have to help others. I am grateful that I continue to be a voice for children and our planet and for the truth. **What will it take for folks to notice that our planet is burning up ?** I am grateful that I can see, **visually and morally !**

"I learned a long time ago, the wisest thing I can do is to be on my own side." Maya Angelou

"Living in a state of gratitude is the gateway to grace." Arianna Huffington

22 - Valued by GOD
Ignored, Mistreated & Invisible

"Small minds can't comprehend big spirits. To be great, you have to be willing to be mocked, hated, and misunderstood. Stay strong." Anonymous

One of my childhood memories is moving all the time and never having roots or belonging. When we returned from Africa and moved to Midwest City, Oklahoma, I attended a church youth group. I was 10 years old. I rarely talked, but I always helped. The lady in charge of the group kept calling me Kathy as she would ask me to help her with task after task. I helped, but I never corrected her about calling me the wrong name. I figured that it didn't matter. We would be moving again soon. I didn't really belong.

"Let them judge you. Let them misunderstand you. Let them gossip about you. Their opinions aren't your problems. You stay kind, committed to love and free in your authenticity. No matter what they do or say, don't you doubt your worth or the beauty of your truth. Just keep shining like you always do." Scott Stabile

When one is a **single, handicapped, visually-impaired senior woman**, you are more of a target for the ignorant beings that share this planet and want to terrorize others or to prey upon another. Evil folks seem to know which folks are vulnerable. Ungodly folks refuse to look at their own flaws, or to strive to be better people. They are self-centered and mean-spirited. They are always on the look out to take advantage of someone else. These immoral folks will face their weaknesses when they pass through the door of death. These folks had choices, but decided to make the world a more difficult place for those around them, rather than offering a helping hand. A spiteful person makes a neighborhood hateful or unpleasant. They have no honor or virtue. These wicked people are loud, gossipy liars, and want everyone to notice them and their power. They are young souls that have forgotten God.

"If it is an extraordinary blindness to live without investigating what we are, it is a terrible one to live an evil life, while believing in God." Blaise Pascal

"No one escapes this life without scars." Michelle Griep

The goal is to accept your hurt and pain and to still have an open heart.

"Faith and beliefs are common things in all religions, so God is the faith and the belief without exception." Devasish Mridha

I am an introvert. **It isn't easy being God's messenger** - after all, people didn't believe Jesus and he was God's son. I am certainly less ordained and very imperfect. I have no idea why God would choose me to be one of his messengers. I think God does appreciate that I live by my four core values and that I walk my talk. God seems to select humble/meek souls.

"There is no worship for God without the honor of fellow man." Sunday Adelaja

23 - Gratitude and RESILIENCE !

Love

"To speak gratitude is courteous and pleasant, to enact gratitude is generous and noble, but to live gratitude is to touch Heaven."
Johannes A. Gaertner

Triumphs over pain; physical & emotional. <u>**Gratitude is the resilience of the soul.**</u> No matter how difficult things are, there is always something to be thankful for. With my long history of abuse, medical issues, and twelve eye surgeries; my regular daily blessings that I say out loud are thankfulness for: **being able to see**, **being mobile** (even with a cane), **speaking the truth**, **having healthy food**, and **having a comfortable bed in a safe home**. And, with my nerve damage from autonomic neuropathy, I am so very grateful **for indoor plumbing** and **for toilet paper**. **Jonathan**, my only child, and our dog, **Mindy**, are daily blessings as well. Since I live with them, I am blessed to see them daily. Like you, I have wishes; but I do not have needs. I live simply and appreciate everything I have. I am grateful, thankful and helpful.

"Gratitude turns what we have into enough." Aesop

I wish I had been blessed with a grandchild. I have devoted my entire life to children and making the world better for them. Most of my friends my age, in life and on Facebook, have grandchildren and even great grandchildren. I see their delightful pictures and hear their stories regularly. This is one joy that I will never experience personally. And, so it is.
I have dreamed about the wonders of having a loving marriage. This is also not one of my blessings.
However, **I can see well enough to garden, to cook, to**

swim, to paint, and **to write this book.** I am blessed. It is an inside job to remind myself daily about these blessings I have, and to work on overcoming worry, pain, and disappointment. Like me, you have to fill up your own soul daily with gratitude. You can become your own strength. **There is such comfort in gratefulness.**

> **"Gratitude and Attitude are not challenges; they are choices."** Robert Braathe

> **"It's not happiness that brings us gratitude. It's gratitude that brings us happiness."** Anonymous

Everyone, especially those blessed with a long life, experience hardships and heartbreak. We all face the challenges of grief and losses and struggles. Relief is within each of us. When we focus on our blessings rather than our losses, gratitude renews our hope and uplifts our spirit.

> **"Gratitude is Happiness doubled by wonder."**
> G.K. Chesterton

Dogs -- DOG is GOD spelled backward, no surprise to me. I have always felt like dogs were furry angels. They seem to bless people wherever they are.

If you have been blessed to have a dog as part of your family then you know what joy, love, and comfort they can bring to you. Dogs have been especially important to my son. He does not have friends, and he doesn't like people. Jonathan likes one small dog at a time. Jonathan kisses Mindy good night every night; I only get a side hug.

"The best therapist has fur and four legs." Goldenstars

Luckily, I have always had a dog in Jonathan's life. He has been blessed to know real love from three wonderful dogs: Rascal, Dolly, and now Mindy. Dolly and Mindy were rescue dogs. However, they have given us more than the good home we provided them. Jonathan's only time to go outside is when he walks Mindy - or rather she walks him. Jonathan allows Mindy to go wherever she wants to go.

Mindy, 7 year old Shorkie.

"Dogs leave pawprints on our hearts." Dog quote

During COVID, Jonathan started working from home. He got a desk chair for Mindy so she could sit beside him while he worked when he wasn't able to put her in his lap. If you do not feel like you are loved; **get a dog !** If you are lonely; **get a dog !** Mindy gives Jonathan the love that no human could. A dog is such a joy-filled happy creature. A dog is all about giving you love and sharing your life. They depend upon you and appreciate you.

"You can always find hope in a dog's eyes."
Pawsh-Magazine

Dogs help you see nature in new and beautiful ways. They force you to go outside. It is too bad that dogs don't live longer.

"No matter how little money and how few possessions you own, having a dog makes you feel rich." Louis Sabin

"Home is where the dog runs to greet you."
Good Housekeeping

We are meant to share this world with animals. Lucky souls share their homes with an animal or animals.

"The assumption that animals are without rights, and the illusion that our treatment of them has no moral significance, is a positively outrageous example of Western crudity and barbarity. Universal compassion is the only guarantee of morality." Arthur Schopenhauer, philosopher

24 - Fear and Secret
Insecurity, & Disorder - Where is GOD ???

Most every person who has been blessed to live a long life has probably known fear, insecurity, and disorder. This is especially true if you are a single woman; and even more so, if you are a single, handicapped senior woman. Being a senior dealing with major medical issues can be a lonely, terrifying experience, especially dealing with sight issues.

After a birthday drama, I sent this note to my Painting Group - I was feeling very unsupported by them through my scary walk to avoid blindness. I thought VISUAL people might understand, not so. They were more concerned about their birthdays than about my sight.

I am the only one who has had eight major eye surgeries and four knee procedures in the last two and a half years. For my stem cell and PRP knee procedures, each time I was on the couch with my knee elevated and iced for four days. Then, I was on a walker for a week. I am also the only member of the group that has three or four medical appointments every week. Just because I don't whine and don't ask for help, doesn't mean that I am not suffering and that I don't need peace to heal. I have no more to give. I wish each of you could have walked my walk for just one week. I have planned and executed your birthday celebrations, now I am leaving the Painting Group.

Clearly, I was no longer in a good place to be a friend in this group. I am sure you have felt abandoned like this as well, probably for another reason. However, the loneliness is the same. The sadness is the same. The fear and insecurity are the same. Where are people

111

when you need understanding, comfort and support ?
Where is God ?

In times like these, I find that I have to be still and look within - **find peace within myself**. I have to reach for my soul and know God is stillness. Then, I have to struggle to wait for the answer. Sometimes the answer isn't what I want to hear - like leave the Painting Group. However, you need to do what is best for your health, your growth, and your peace.

> **"With God, all things are possible."** Bill Graham

I have known so many things that I wish I hadn't known - abuse, hunger, homelessness. I remember riding a bus from Bloomington, Indiana to Chicago with only twenty-five cents in my pocket - not even enough to buy a snack at a rest stop. You can survive it all.

In the stillness, find your path. Your soul will guide you to your goal. And, with each experience, learn what you need to learn so that you don't have to repeat your lesson. Respect and honor yourself, even when others don't. It is in this place of stillness that you will find GOD.

> **"It doesn't matter where you came from, it doesn't matter how poor you are, it doesn't matter where your family was. It all doesn't matter. You can achieve anything if you have really clear goals and if your work really hard to learn what you need to learn."**
> Brain Tracy

In spite of my very humble beginnings, I did earn a college degree in Education; and, later a Master's Degree in Education. I worked incredibly hard, so my education has great value to me. I even have fifty-six graduate Science hours beyond my Master's Degree. And now, having taught for 35 full time years, I have a decent retirement.

I sometimes ask where is God when I see folks my age with grandchildren. I have devoted my whole life to children; yet, I have only one child and no grandchildren. Sometimes, as hard as you try or as deeply as you desire; the answer is NO. However, you will never know unless you try. And, if the answer is NO, you have to focus upon your other blessings. In my case, I have had twelve major eye surgeries, and thanks to amazing doctors, **I can still see.** THIS IS A GREAT BLESSING. All over the world, folks with my rare eye condition are blind.

"It doesn't matter where you start, only that you begin." Robin Sharma

My friend, this is your fun bonus for reading my book and honoring me with your willingness to listen to me. **We all want to be heard.**

"Write something so painfully personal you pray nobody reads it." —Chad Gervich

MY SECRET - Luke is tall (6'4"), dark, handsome and every woman's dream of sexy masculinity in the prime of his life. His dark eyes express what his words rarely say. They can be soft with kindness and concern. They deepen with lust, desire and hunger. They harden cold

113

with disapproval and anger. Sometimes, his eyes are even scary, like looking into the face of Satan. Luke's eyes are the window to his soul and to his unspoken words. He is the envy of every man in the locker room. I am short (5'1"), dumpy, and cute - a feisty curly head with pale Scotch-Irish freckled skin. Luke has well-tanned skin. He often says, when we are skin-to-skin, that we look like we are two different races. My eyes dance with delight, hope, and mischief. I laugh easily and smile often; yet inside, I am usually afraid.

He is confident and serious. Luke is very muscular and incredibly strong. He picks me up easily, as if I were only a five-pound sack of potatoes. Luke has school loans, a mortgage, and a car payment. I am the proud mother of one wonderful son. Luke has never been married. I have had two failed marriages. Luke is bravely independent; believing he needs no one. I long to belong. Luke is a competent, compassionate PA - physician's assistant; I am a fun-loving retired Science teacher, now a Watercolor Artist. He is in the prime of his life; I am a full of life 75 years old senior, slowed by a cane and eye surgeries. We met at a medical talk on the UNCA campus. We have been secret lovers since 2012.

I am a gardener - for the pollinators, especially the bees; and I am an artist. I am very vocal as a political activist for children and for our planet. However, my personal life is private. I drive a blue Subaru Forester with a handicapped license plate. My vehicles are always blue. For several years, my Subaru was covered in Bernie Sanders' magnets while I campaigned. I am a flaming liberal. Luke is also a liberal, like Jesus.

We are both drawn to trees and water. We love playing in a shower together. I swim daily; Luke kayaks often and every year goes on a two-week camping river trip on a river in our western United States. When

114

Luke was on his River Trip this past summer, he saw first-hand the wildfires that are burning up our west. We both value wildlife, wild places, and our environment. I am dedicated to leaving a living world to the children. Our core values of honesty, service and liberalism are aligned. We have both had non-relation homeless people live with us for over six months. We care about our fellow human beings. Intelligence is very sexy to us.

Luke, a former Marine, had lived many adventuresome lives before settling into Medical School. He received his PA (Physician's Assistant) degree in 2010 from South Carolina. In late 2011, he moved to Asheville. Luke lives a life as an amazing athlete, accomplished as a daring mountain biker, a fearless white water rapids kayaker, and a dare-devil skier in Colorado. He has a large circle of active camping, kayaking and biking friends. Otherwise, Luke lives his life privately. The women in his office work daily to uncover the secrets and the mysteries of his life. I like Luke best when he is clean-shaven. He is always buzzed cut around his head. When he grows a beard for winter skiing, it is full and scratchy. Luke's most recent huge projects have been remodeling his east Asheville log home which had turned him into a hermit for a number of years. He is a self-taught handyman who can remodel or repair anything in this home. Luke even repairs his vehicles. He is a hard-working man with great style and set passions. Luke drives a white Subaru Outback. His vehicles are always white. Luke is my secret lover.

I call him Handsome and he calls me Sexy. He also calls me WW for Wild Woman, Wonderful Woman, or Wacky Wild depending on the text message. Sometimes he calls me Baby, Baby. We call each other Lover. He says that I am **"the one consistent person in his life who tries to understand and to love him"**. We are soulmates.

When I decided to move to Durham to be closer to my son. Luke asked me to marry him and to stay in Asheville. I was honored and thrilled; however, I loved him too much to saddle a vibrant daring athlete with an old woman having many medical issues and being handicapped. In my heart, I wanted to stay in Asheville and to be with Luke. In my head, I knew that I needed to move to Durham to be closer to my son and to the medical care I needed for my rare conditions, especially for my vision issues. It was with a heavy heart that I made the move to Durham.

Luke and I are still very connected. We feel that we were lovers in a previous life and that we will be lovers again in our next life. Our souls are connected. We feel that we are older souls. Luke is 25 years younger than I am. Both having Science backgrounds, even with a large age difference, we can both talk about anything, even body parts. Our communication is very open and honest. No topic is ever off limits. Our communication is real and deep. Luke is kinder than I am about human imperfections. He seems to always see the good in others. With age, I am impatient and judgmental. I feel the burning need to speak up for children and for this planet, as Jesus directed me to do. Humans and our society are leaving too few resources and too many major problems for the next generation. People have not taken care of Earth.

One of the ways Luke and I stay connected is that I track him daily. I know when he is at work. I know if he goes hiking or mountain biking after clinic hours. I even track him on his western river adventures. A couple of times my tracking has helped him as he regularly goes on solo adventures. We also text daily. Tracking gives us more to text about. Plus, we send photos back and forth regularly. Sometimes we chat on the phone on his morning drive to work as he has a long commute. We make an effort to stay connected daily.

Since moving to Durham, Jonathan knows about Luke.

I share my Luke story so that you know that some souls are connected for several human experiences; soulmates. When you look at couples that don't appear to belong together, consider that they may have been together in previous lifetimes as well.

I have been on dating websites off and on for 22 years looking for a guy my own age. Men my age don't even bother to respond to me. They are looking for younger women with money. I am just another short, dumpy, curly headed senior woman with a cute smile. And, for many, I am too liberal and I don't fit their double standards. After all, few men are brave enough to have their beliefs challenged. Little do these men know that I am a very passionate woman and lots of fun to be with. As Luke once wrote to me, **"You are the most fun, free-spirited woman that I have ever known"**. I guess most men just don't know a great woman when they see her. Too bad, I am also very appreciative - something many women lack.

25 - LIVING LIBERAL, like JESUS

"The secret of FREEDOM lies in educating people, whereas the secret of tyranny is keeping them ignorant." Maximilien Robespierre

We need more FREE state and community colleges and more FREE trade schools in America.

"Jesus was not killed by atheism and anarchy. He was brought down by law and order allied with religion - which is always a deadly mix. Beware those who claim to know the will of God and are prepared to use force, if necessary, to make others conform. Beware those who cannot tell God's will from their own." Rev. Dr. Barbara Brown Taylor

If you think I am TOO LIBERAL, just wait until you meet JESUS. Have you noticed how you have two ears and one mouth ? I always told my students that this is so that you listen twice as much as you talk. Listening is your opportunity to observe and to see the truth for yourself. Young souls want to talk and not listen. They often loudly have to be the center of any discussion. Old souls are wiser and listen well.

"Long ago, there was a noble word, LIBERAL, which derives from the word free. Now a strange thing happened to that word. A man named HITLER made it a term of abuse, a matter of suspicion, because those who were not with him were against him, and Liberals had no use for Hitler. And then another man named McCarthy cast the same opprobrium on the word ...... We must cherish and honor the word free or it will cease to apply to us." Eleanor Roosevelt

"The word LISTEN contains the same letters as the word SILENT." Alfred Brendel

"The story of Christ as an adult is beautiful. He owned nothing. He healed the sick. He helped without expecting anything in return. He was, for all intents and purposes, a Socialist. And I love that. If we could all love as he did, not judging one another, but helping each other, feeding each other, caring about EVERY person without worrying about size, race, sex, financial standing, diffability, sexual orientation, etc...what a wonderful world this would be. You know. Just be kind and keep your nose where it belongs...on your own face, in your in business. One can dream..." Cyndi Lou Ammons

If you don't speak the truth and speak up for the truth, the TRUTH will be lost. My **four CORE VALUES** are and have always been: **HONESTY, JUSTICE/FAIRNESS; GENEROSITY;** and **SERVICE**. I think Jesus could relate to them.

"Never be afraid to raise your voice for honesty and truth and compassion against injustice and lying and greed. If people all over the world would do this, it would change the earth." William Faulkner

What we allow to go unaddressed, goes uncorrected.

"In life, it's important to know when to stop arguing with people and simply let them be wrong."
Brian Weiner

Right is always right; wrong is always wrong. Even knowing this, sometimes I have to stop speaking up; people are set in their beliefs and few are open-minded enough to consider change, even to save their own soul. I understand what Jesus meant.

26 - I AM ETERNAL; YOU ARE ETERNAL !

As a retired Science teacher, I know that our bodies are made of elements; mostly hydrogen, oxygen, carbon, nitrogen, sulfur, and phosphorus; mostly in the form of water. This is 99% of our body. We are **matter** and **energy**. Having survived a near death experience, I know that our soul is made up of **everlasting energy**. Humans are made of stardust. We share the same elements as stars, but in different amounts. Humans and their galaxy have 97% of the same kind of atoms. These are often referred to as THE ELEMENTS OF LIFE. These elements are not lost; they can become units in different forms when our body dies.

When a body dies, it naturally begins to decompose. Nature has an amazing system in place for the human body to decay and the elements to be dispersed naturally back into Nature. The microbes and the bacteria in and on the body do this work immediately and naturally. Bodies aren't meant to be embalmed and to be put into caskets. Nature has a system already in place to recycle the body back into Nature. The elements aren't lost, just reused.

As for the soul, at the time of death, it leaves the body and crosses over into the spirit world through the **doorway of death**. **THE SOUL IS ETERNAL. MY SOUL IS ETERNAL. YOUR SOUL IS ETERNAL.** The soul spends time on the other side of the human experience waiting to return to the human world. Depending upon how the human life was lived, the soul has a blissful or a terrifying visit in the spirit world. In my case, I was blessed with a wonderfully joyous, heavenly visit to the spirit world. I didn't want to return to the human world or to the human experience.

121

YOU ARE A SPIRIT HAVING A HUMAN EXPERIENCE. Your soul left the spirit world to be born into a human experience. Many believe that you have chosen the human experience that you are going to have. Each of us is on a journey. We are on our own journey of learning. We each have angels that can help and assist us during our earthly experience, if we ask. We all have gifts that we can use while we are on earth to make the world a better place. If we evolve enough, together we could create **Heaven on Earth**.

A **young soul** is someone who has had fewer human experiences. They are usually easy to spot. They enter a room and demand attention immediately. When they attend a presentation, they keep interrupting the presenter. A young soul is like an undisciplined child who demands constant devotion. This soul strives to be noticed before all else. A young soul is often loud and boisterous which is one of the ways they draw attention to themselves. It can be difficult to learn with a young soul around for they constantly create distractions which bring attention back to them. They speak loudly so that everyone will notice them. Young souls can also create unrest and fear by the criminal means they use to get attention. These are humans who are still finding their place in the world. They can be competitive, materialistic, and ambitious. Young souls usually feel like they are always right. Life is often a contest. Entertainers are young souls. They thrive being in the spotlight.

An **old soul** is someone who has had many human experiences and who has become wiser and less self-centered from their previous experiences. They have evolved. As children they are immediately seen as intelligent. These humans (people) are usually less materialistic and more caring of animals and other humans, especially children. They are people who walk their talk and who **quietly** live as a model for others. These special souls are guides as to how humans should be living. They rarely look for attention or praise. These are people who experience their own divinity by being still and hearing their inner voice, their heart, and their intuition. These are souls that have learned to be silent and to find their own sanctuary within themselves. These older souls have simple needs and do not wish to accumulate possessions. They focus on meaningful connections and need time alone. They are usually empathic and feel like they belong to a different time. Old souls are rare. They know how to live and how to love completely. You will find them volunteering in soup kitchens, at food banks, and in environmental groups. They have evolved beyond their ego. Givers are older souls. They are grateful, thankful, and helpful.

"When it comes to life the critical thing is whether you take things for granted or take them with gratitude."
G. K. Chesterton

Recently I attended a senior event and sat at a table with four other seniors. I didn't know three of the people. One woman totally dominated the conversation talking about her three cats and her dog. She clearly is a young soul even though she is a senior. This woman had no interest in any of the rest of us. She was totally self-absorbed and self-centered. This is how I often view folks, as young or old souls. Any time someone dominates a conversation, they are clearly a young soul no matter their age. Older souls tend to be listeners. They talk less and when they do, they show interest in other people. **Are you a younger or an older soul ?**

"Too often we underestimate the power of a touch, a smile, a kind word, a listening ear, an honest compliment, or the smallest act of caring, all of which have the potential to turn a life around." Leo Buscaglia

Proverbs 17:28   **"Even a fool who keeps silent is considered wise; when he closes his lips, he is deemed intelligent."**

These old souls can be compared to the life of Jesus - **humble, content,** and **faithful.** This is sometimes referred to as having a **MEEK spirit.** When a soul evolves into an old, wise soul, this spirit may decide to stay in the spirit world and to not continue to have human experiences. This spirit will reside in the blissful spirit world - the world which many of us call **Heaven.**

"If the only prayer you ever say in your life is "thank you" that would suffice." Meister Eckhart

Always be GRATEFUL, THANKFUL, and HELPFUL.

"GRATITUDE is a simple, but powerful thing." Randy Pausch

In this book, I have tried to follow the wise words of Jesus and of Mahatma Gandhi - "…. **be the change you wish to see in the world** …" These wise words of Gandhi's have been on my refrigerator since my 1998 Jesus encounters. In my book I have tried to speak the truth and fulfill my directive from Jesus. Wherever you are in your growth as a soul, **YOU ARE ETERNAL.**

I am eternal; YOU ARE ETERNAL !

May you be aware of your blessings and your angels.

When one is visually impaired, there is much time
to think reflectively and to be grateful.

These Old Hands ....
by P Diane Chambers

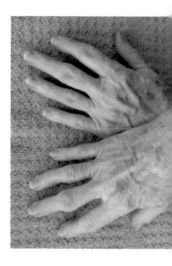

*Homage to my OLD HANDS, so much
work - no longer pretty; yet, with
history & character.*

These old hands have toiled in the clay
soil;
Planted, weeded, pruned, and prayed for
rain.

These old hands have lived in 37
    different homes;
Packing, moving, making beds, and cleaning - a strain.

These old hands have been to class and taught in schools;
    They have been blessed to witness learning gain.

These old hands have been privileged to hold many other hands;
    Babies, children, teens, and seniors in the slow lane.

These old hands have tried to share and to help others;
    A passionate life-time goal - still working to attain.

These old hands have sweated for our pollinators;
    Volunteering, donating, planting, and campaigns.

These old hands have labored for future generations;
    Donating, voting, meeting - hoping to inspire - a drain.

These old hands have loved to draw and to paint;
    Supporting notice of Mother Nature's struggle - in vain.

These old hands have known RA, cancer, and other medicals;
    Doctors, hospitals, surgeries, inflammation, and pain.

These old hands have so much more work to do;
    Plant, cook, weed, donate, swim - trying not to complain.

As Stephen Hawking said, **"Intelligence is the ability to adapt to change."**

"Life is either a daring adventure or nothing at all."
Helen Keller

May I inspire you in my imperfection. 😊

"Each Day comes bearing its gifts. Untie the ribbon."
Ann Ruth Schabacker

"JOY does not simply happen to us. We have to choose joy and keep choosing it every day."
Henri Nouwen

Proceeds from this book will go to Digdeep.org --
WATER IS LIFE !!! There are 2.2 million Americans who still do not have running water in their homes. Much of the work of Dig Deep is in the Navajo and Appalachian areas of America. **Running water changes lives forever.**